The Decline and Fall of IBM

End of an American Icon?

by

ROBERT X CRINGELY

THE DECLINE AND FALL OF IBM

End of an American Icon?

Published by NeRDTV, LLC

Formatted by Any Subject Books, London

Paperback edition: ISBN 978-0-9904444-2-8

Epub edition: ISBN 978-0-9904444-1-1

Mobi (Kindle) edition: ISBN 978-0-9904444-0-4

In memory of Lois Cringely

1924-2014

CONTENTS

Preface

Introduction

Chapter One

Chapter Two

Chapter Three

PREFACE

When I was growing up in Ohio, ours was the only house in the neighborhood with a laboratory. In it, the previous owner, Leonard Skeggs, had invented the automated blood analyzer, which pretty much created the present biomedical industry. Unwilling to let such a facility go to waste, I threw myself into research. It was 1961 and I was 8 years old.

I was always drawn to user interface design and quickly settled, as Gene Roddenberry did in *Star Trek* half a decade later, on the idea of controlling computers with voice. My father was a natural scrounger, and using all the cool crap he dragged home from who knows where, I decided to base my voice control work on the amplitude modulation optical sound track technology from 16mm film (we had a projector). If I could paint optical tracks to represent commands then all I'd need was some way of characterizing and analyzing those tracks to tell the computer what to do. But the one thing I didn't have down in the lab in 1961 was a computer.

That's what took me to IBM.

I wrote a letter to IBM CEO T.J. Watson, Jr., pecking it out on an old Underwood manual typewriter. My proposal was simple: a 50/50 partnership between IBM and me to develop and exploit advanced user interface technologies. In a few days I received a letter from IBM. I don't know if it was from Watson, himself, because neither my parents nor I thought to keep the letter. The response invited me to a local IBM research facility to discuss my plan.

I wore a suit, of course, on that fateful day. My dad drove me in his 1959 Chrysler New Yorker that was foggy with blue cigarette smoke. He dropped me at the curb and told me he'd be back in a couple of hours. Inside the IBM building I met with six engineers, all dressed in dark suits with the skinny ties of that era, the tops of their socks showing when they sat down. They took me very seriously. T.J. Watson had called the meeting, himself.

Nobody said, "Wait a minute, you're 8."

I made my pitch, which they absorbed in silence. Then they introduced me to their interface of choice, the punched card.

Uh-oh.

Thirty years later, long after he retired, I got to know Homer Sarasohn, IBM's chief engineer at the time of my meeting. When I told him the story of my experience with IBM, he almost fell off his chair laughing. My ideas were good, Homer said, they were just forty years too early. In other words, they were still 10 years in the future when Homer and I were talking a decade ago.

The message that came through clearly from those IBMers back in 1961 was that they were a little embarrassed by their own lack of progress. Terminals weren't even common at that point, but they were coming. If I could have offered IBM a more practical magic bullet, I think they might have grabbed it.

So when I write about IBM and you wonder where I am coming from, it's at least in part from that boyhood experience. A huge company took me seriously for a morning, and quite possibly changed my life in the process.

Alas, that IBM no longer exists. So I had to write this book in an attempt to get it back.

INTRODUCTION

The story of this book began in the summer of 2007 when I was shooting a TV documentary called *The Transformation Age – Surviving a Technology Revolution*, at the Mayo Clinic in Rochester, Minnesota. Rochester has two main employers, Mayo and IBM, and a reporter can't spend several days in town without hearing a lot about both. What I heard about IBM was very disturbing. Huge layoffs were coming as IBM tried to transfer much of its U.S. services business directly to lower-cost countries like India and Argentina. It felt to me like a step down in customer service, and from what I heard the IBMers weren't being treated well either. And yet there was nothing about it even in the local press.

I've been a professional journalist for more than forty years and my medium of choice these days is the Internet where I am a blogger. Bloggers like me are the 21st century version of newspaper beat reporters. Only bloggers have the patience (or obsessive compulsive disorder) to follow one company every day. The traditional business press doesn't tend to follow companies closely enough to really understand the way they work, nor do they stay long enough to see emerging trends. Today business news is all about executive personalities, mergers and acquisitions, and of course quarterly earnings.

The only time a traditional reporter bothers to look — really look — inside a company is if they have a book contract, and that is rare. But I've been banging away at this story for seven years.

Starting in 2007, during that trip to Minnesota, I saw troubling things at IBM. I saw the company changing, and not for the better. I saw the people of IBM (they are actually called "resources") beginning to lose faith in their company and starting to panic. I wrote story after story, and IBM workers called or wrote me, both to confirm my fears and to give me even more material.

I was naive. My hope was that when it became clear to the public what was happening at IBM that things would change. Apparently I was the only member of the press covering the story in any depth — sometimes the only one at all. I was sure the national press, or at least the trade press, would jump on this story as I wrote it. Politicians would notice. The grumbling of more than a million IBM retirees would bring the story more into public discourse. Shamed, IBM would reverse course and change behavior. None of that happened. This lack of deeper interest in IBM boggled my mind, and still does.

Even on the surface, IBM in early 2014 looks like a troubled company. Sales are flat to down, and earnings are too. More IBM customers are probably unhappy with Big Blue right now than are happy. After years of corporate downsizing, employee morale is at an all-time low. Bonuses and even annual raises are rare. But for all that, IBM is still an enormous multinational corporation with high profits, deep pockets, and grand ambitions for new technical initiatives in cloud computing, Big Data analytics, and artificial intelligence as embodied in the company's *Jeopardy* game-show-winning Watson technology. Yet for all this, IBM seems to have lost some of its mojo, or at least that's what Wall Street and the business analysts are starting to think.

Just *starting* to think? The truth is that IBM is in deep trouble and has been since before the Great Recession of 2008. The company has probably been doomed since 2010. It's just that nobody knew it. These are harsh words, I know, and I don't write them lightly. By doomed I mean that IBM has chosen a path that, if unchanged, can only lead to decline, corporate despair, and ultimately insignificance for what was once the mightiest of American businesses.

If I am correct about IBM, whose fault is it?

In its 100 years of existence, the International Business Machines Company has had just nine chief executive officers. Two of those CEOs, Thomas J. Watson, and his son, Thomas J. Watson Jr., served for 57 of those 100 years. Between father and son they created the first true multinational computer company, and defined what information technology meant for business in the 20th century. But the 20th century is over and with it the old IBM. In the current century, IBM has had three CEOs: Louis V. Gerstner Jr., Samuel J. Palmisano, and Virginia M. Rometty. They have redefined Big Blue, changing its personality in the process. Some of this change was very good, some of it was inevitable, but much of it was bad. This book is about that new personality and about that process.

Lou Gerstner saved IBM from a previous crisis in the 1990s, and then went on to set the company up for the crisis of today. Gerstner was a great leader who made important changes in IBM, but didn't go far enough. Worse still, he made a few strategic errors that helped the company into its current predicament. Sam Palmisano reversed some of the good that Gerstner had done and compounded what Gerstner did wrong. The current crisis was made inevitable on Palmisano's watch. New CEO Ginni Rometty will probably take the fall for the mistakes of her predecessors. She simply hasn't been on the job long enough to have been responsible for such a mess. But she's at least partly to blame because she also hasn't done anything — *anything* — to fix it.

We'll get to the details in a moment, but first here is an e-mail I received this January from a complete stranger at IBM. I have since confirmed the identity of this person. He or she is exactly as described. Some of the terminology may go over your head, but by the end of the book you'll understand it all. Read it here and then tell me there's nothing wrong at IBM.

"Please keep this confidential as to who I am, because I'm going to tell you the inside scoop you cannot get. I am rated as a #1. That's as high as you go, so calling me a disgruntled employee won't work.

"Right now the pipeline is dry — the number of services folks on the bench is staggering and the next layoff is coming. The problem now is that the frequent rebalancing has destroy1ed morale, and so worried troops don't perform well. Having taken punitive rather than thoughtful actions, Ginni has gutted the resources required to secure new business. Every B-School graduate learns not to do that. The result is a dry pipeline, and while you can try to blame the cloud for flagging sales, that doesn't work. Those cloud data centers are growing. The demand for hardware didn't shrink — it simply moved. Having eliminated what did not seem necessary, the brains and strategy behind the revenue are now gone, leaving only 'do now' perform people who cannot sell. Sales reps have no technical resources and so they cannot be effective. Right now we cannot sell. There is no one to provide technical support. The good people are finding jobs elsewhere. The [job] market outside IBM is improving. I am interviewing at a dozen companies now. Soon as I find something perfect for me, I'm gone. They don't expect people like me to leave.

"Ever work anywhere where you were afraid to make a large purchase like a car because you don't know that you will have a job in a month? That's how everyone feels at IBM. Now we are doing badly on engagements. I cannot think of a single engagement where we are not in trouble. We lay off key people in the middle of major commitments. I cannot tell you how many times I've managed to get involved in an engagement and cannot lay my hands on the staff required to perform.

"The whole idea that people in different time zones, all over the world can deliver on an engagement in Chicago is absurd.

"Lastly, using the comparative scheme for employee evaluations is simply stupid. No matter how great the entire staff is, a stack ranking will result in someone at the top and someone at the bottom. It ignores that the dead wood is gone.

"Ginni has made one horrible mistake. Sam, and now, Ginni, has forgotten that IBM was made by its people. They have failed to understand their strongest assets, and shortly will pay for that. IBM just hit the tipping point. I do not think there is any way back."

Years ago IBM could sell an idea. They'd come in, manage a project, develop an application, and it would make a big difference to the customer. IBM would generally deliver on their promises, and those benefits more than paid for the high cost of the project and the computers. IBM transformed banks by getting them off ledger books. Remember the term "bankers' hours?" Banks were only open to the public for part of the day. The rest of the time was spent with the doors closed, reconciling the transactions.

But that was then and this is now. IBM's performance on its accounts over the last 10 years has damaged the company's reputation. Customers no longer trust IBM to manage projects well, get the projects finished, or have the projects work as promised. IBM is now hard pressed to properly support what they sell. Those ten years have traumatized IBM. Its existing businesses are under performing, and its new businesses are at risk of not succeeding because the teams that will do the work are damaged.

Let's look to the top of IBM to understand how this happened.

"The importance of managers being aligned with shareholders — not through risk-free instruments like stock options, but through the process of putting their own money on the line through direct ownership of the company — became a critical part of the management philosophy I brought to IBM," claims former CEO Lou Gerstner in his book, *Who Says Elephants Can't Dance?*

Defying (or perhaps learning from) Gerstner, IBM's leaders today are fully isolated and immune from the long-term consequences of their decisions. People who own companies manage them to be viable for the long term. IBM's leaders do not.

I am not going to explain in this introduction what is wrong with IBM. I have the whole book to do that. But I do want to use this space to explain why a book even needs to be written and how I came up with that provocative title.

The book had to be written because writing the same story over and over for seven years hasn't changed anything. The only possible way to still accomplish that, I figured, was to put all I know about IBM in one place, lead readers through the story, and at the end take a shot at explaining how to actually fix IBM. The last chapter goes into some detail on how to get IBM back on course. It isn't too late for that, though time is growing short.

The title is based on Edward Gibbon's *The History of the Decline and Fall of the Roman Empire*, published in six volumes beginning in 1776. *Decline and Fall* was the first modern book on Roman history. It was relatively objective and drawn from primary sources. And it recounted the fall of an empire some thought would last forever. In industrial terms many people thought the same about IBM.

Gibbon's thesis was that the Roman Empire fell prey to barbarian invasions because of a loss of virtue. The Romans became weak over time, outsourcing the defense of their empire to barbarian mercenaries who eventually took over. Gibbon saw this Praetorian Guard as the cause of decay, abusing their power through imperial assassinations and incessant demands for more pay.

The Praetorian Guard appears to be in charge these days at IBM, as you'll see.

Even a self-published book with one author is the product of many minds. Katy Gurley and Michael McCarthy were my editors. Kara Westerman copy-edited the book. Lars Foster designed the cover. Many loyal IBMers gave me both information and the benefit of their wisdom to make the book possible. Out of necessity, because quoting them directly would imperil their jobs, these heroes must go unnamed.

We can all hope their assistance will not have been in vain.

1

GOOD OLD IBM

Few of us actually live in the present. Our minds are often in the recent past where judgments are formed and go for long periods of time unchallenged. That's why the IBM nearly everyone thinks of is the IBM of the Watsons, father and son. That IBM — of the 1960s and 1970s — was less a company than it was a *country*. In some ways it still is. IBM has a greater gross national product than most countries. It has some 430,000 workers. Throw in spouses and their kids and we're looking at well over a million citizens of IBM.

Twenty years ago, IBM was demographically most like Kuwait, but temperamentally IBM was like Switzerland. Like Switzerland, IBM traditionally had been conservative, a little dull, and slow to change, yet prosperous. Both countries were in the habit of taking in more money than they gave out. Both countries learned slowly and adapted at their own pace. Switzerland and IBM could survive anything, or at least thought they could. They may have been slow, but you didn't mess with them, because they fought to keep what was theirs. And if pushed, they'd fight dirty.

Like Switzerland, IBM was landlocked, though Big Blue's barriers were regulation and internal rivalries, not geography. IBM was surrounded by US antitrust laws and by a now-defunct 1956 consent decree that somewhat limited its ability to wreak havoc upon the land. Even more limiting was the rivalry between IBM's different computer divisions, each protecting its turf from incursions by the others. There was no law or consent decree limiting the amount of infighting that went on within the company.

The citizens of IBM didn't invent the computer. They never made the most powerful computers either. Back then, the citizens of IBM just made more computers than anybody else. So, just as Levi's defined blue jeans to a world that somehow survived Gloria Vanderbilt, IBM defined computers.

IBM computers didn't stand apart, but IBM people did. Of all the companies I've dealt with, the only two whose people consistently presented a common front, a kind of unique company style, were those from IBM and Procter & Gamble. I believe this came from their hiring practices, and the way they indoctrinated their workers — both companies had official songbooks! There must be something very unifying about getting together with a thousand other folks at a sales meeting in New York or Cincinnati and singing your guts out in praise of the Old Man.

The men and women of IBM had their own language. A minicomputer was a *mid-range system*. A monitor was a *display*. A hard disk drive had one or several magnetic platters that spun continuously, yet for some reason was called a *fixed disk* although it wasn't fixed at all. Sticking to these terms preserved the illusion that IBM's $600 dollar display was somehow different from Samsung's $249 monitor; or that IBM's fixed disk drive, made under contract by Seagate, was somehow superior to the exact same drive sold for half that price under the Seagate brand.

Like Rolex or Gucci, IBM knew that they were not really selling computers at all, but the IBM brand. IBM people in those days were a little smug and rarely in a hurry for anything. Most IBMers were hired straight out of college and had never worked for another company. They were folks who drove Buick Regals and took them to the car wash every Saturday morning, paying extra to get the hot wax. Their contented middle-class style bugged the hell out of Silicon Valley entrepreneur types, who wanted to do business with IBM and yet couldn't understand that there were folks in the world — even in the world of computers — who weren't like them, madly driven to make a fortune and own a Ferrari before their midlife crisis.

IBMers just weren't in the business to become millionaires. How could they be? These people weren't sitting on stock options in some start-up, waiting for their penny shares to go public at $8. They worked for a company that went public under the name of Computing

Tabulating Recording Corp. almost 90 years ago.

Even IBM salespeople, who worked on commission selling computers that cost millions of dollars, had carefully set quotas that effectively limited their earning potential. Ross Perot, founder of Electronic Data Systems and later a candidate for President, was one IBM salesman who got fed up and left the company when he filled his sales quota for the entire year by the end of January, and knew that he wouldn't be allowed to sell any more computers — or earn any more money — for eleven more months.

The workers at IBM in those days didn't need to be rich. They either wanted the security of working for a company that would employ them for life, with fringe benefits beyond those of any welfare state, or they wanted the sheer power that came from eventually working up into the stratospheric reaches of what was then the most powerful company on earth. Money and power were not synonymous at IBM, where power was preferred.

The price of both prosperity and power was compliance with the rules and the pace of IBM. The rules said that you went where the company sent you (IBM was said to stand for *I've Been Moved*), did what the company asked you to do, and didn't talk about work with strangers. There is a class of company that won't tolerate different behavior, and those companies sometimes suffer for it. IBM was like that. The pace there was slow because it took time to get 860,000 legs marching together.

At its apex in the mid-1980s, IBM had seventeen layers of management. This in itself is easy to criticize, but, just as dinosaurs were successful for tens of millions of years, IBM was optimized for serving big business and big government customers that typically had as many layers or more. There were layers of management to check and verify each decision as it was made and amended. The safety net was so big at IBM that it was hard to make a bad decision. In fact, it was hard to make any decision at all, which turned out later to be the company's greatest problem and the source of its ultimate decline.

Before beginning each new assignment, for example, IBM people were thoroughly briefed with all the information the company believed they would need to know to do their new job. The briefings were so complete that most IBM people didn't bother to do any outside reading or research on their own. If IBM marketing executives knew how their personal computers compared with the competition's, it was nearly always through their briefing books, and hardly ever by actually using the other guy's hardware—or even their own.

And at the top of IBM, most energy went into playing corporate political games, as though competitors and even the global computer market didn't exist.

It was corporate infighting, in fact, that made entry into the microcomputer market so attractive to IBMers who had grown tired of slugging out the next point of mainframe market share, while at the same time engaging in internecine warfare with other company divisions. In the microcomputer business circa 1980 there looked to be no divisional rivalries to worry about, no antitrust considerations, and, most important, the customers were all new, fresh meat, having never before felt the firm handshake of an IBM sales rep. Every sales dollar brought in from a microcomputer sale would be a dollar that would not otherwise have come to IBM. There was something pure about that, and the IBM executives who led the company's assault on the microcomputer market knew that success on this new battlefield could eventually lead them to the real font of power: IBM worldwide headquarters in Armonk, New York.

With the success of IBM's 360 mainframes the company totally dominated corporate and government IT. The 360, along with IBM's languages *were* IBM's businesses. At the time nothing else mattered and nothing would change that... until of course something did. The problem was that IBM didn't see that something coming.

This is not to say that IBM was devoid of ability or ambition. The company had shown through its history an ability to reinvent itself for each new age of technology. But those great leaps forward came at a cost and each time, whether it was following the IBM 360 mainframe in the 1960s, the System34 and 38 minicomputers of the 1970s, or the IBM PCs of the 1980s, Big Blue would be exhausted for a few years and coast along on the high profit margins it had just earned.

But what if those high margins weren't there? That quickly became the case with IBM's personal computer line, which was a marketing success, but a financial failure.

IBM could defend its markets as long as customers were slower to change than even Big Blue itself. This changed somewhat with the arrival of personal computers, which spread technology to smaller customers, and in the Fortune 500, wrested some power from IT departments and placed it in the hands of departments no longer so awed by the power of the mainframe. It became even worse with the eventual rise of the Internet.

In about 1980, When John Opel was CEO and approved Project Chess — the original IBM personal computer program — the company was primarily a mainframe computer maker. IBM had gone through a huge growth spurt based almost entirely on what the first President Bush would have called "voodoo economics." IBM under Opel began urging its largest mainframe customers to switch from leasing their mainframes to buying them outright, which overnight raised revenue from those customers by 10 times or more. These lease conversions were reportedly the idea of Vice-Chairman and CFO Paul Rizzo. IBM had a huge sales surge as a result, generating cash that made the company look richer than ever; but that money also had to be put to use in the business. What made this voodoo was IBM's stated expectation to analysts that this sales level would be somehow sustainable even after all the leases had been bought out.

By that point, of course, John Opel was gone, having reached 60 — IBM's mandatory retirement age for all CEOs not named *Watson*. John Akers was in as the new CEO, and IBM was becoming better known as a PC company — a PC company that couldn't make a profit.

The reason IBM couldn't make a profit on its PC line came down to overhead, agility, competition, and Microsoft. Companies like Compaq and Dell had lower cost structures than IBM and could make the same or better profit on each PC than IBM could, while still undercutting Big Blue on price. Since all boxes ran the same Microsoft software nothing made IBM's computers intrinsically better. Worse still, those upstart companies could develop new generations of PCs faster than lumbering IBM could.

At one point IBM tried to buy all the Intel 80286 processors on the market, apparently hoping that it could put off competitors by controlling microprocessor supply. Quite the contrary, IBM's move simply forced Compaq to move up to the more powerful 80386 processor, while IBM was stuck trying to use up its existing stock of now-obsolete 286s. As a result, IBM PCs were not only more expensive, they were less powerful too.

Worse still, IBM tried to retake control of the PC market by introducing a new hardware platform — the PS/2 series featuring the MicroChannel bus, or architecture, — and new operating system software in OS/2. The PS/2 line and OS/2 cost billions for IBM to bring to market and therefore cost substantially more than their competition. And, because they were initially hobbled by 286 processors from that previous botched purchasing decision, the PS/2s were less powerful too. Then the PC clone industry decided not to follow IBM this time, which would have involved giving most of their profit to IBM in MicroChannel license fees. IBM had been inclined to push all its PC chips onto the table by eliminating completely its previous and less expensive architecture, but cooler minds prevailed that time and the PC division was saved from itself.

The split between IBM and Microsoft over the Windows development plan and PS/2 was not impacting PC clone sales, either. That meant Microsoft could see that it was no longer dependent on IBM for its success. Any special treatment Microsoft reserved for IBM ended at that point.

If the PC business had been IBM's only problem in 1992, Akers might have survived, but the company was fighting a war on many fronts.

Mainframe lookalikes from Amdahl and Hitachi were undercutting sales at IBM's most important division. Leasing companies were hurting that revenue stream for IBM as a finance engine. This was also the moment when lease-to-sale conversions peaked and then dropped, hurting both revenue and profits. Yet IBM was still heavily investing a fixed percentage of sales in research that couldn't be so flexibly expanded and contracted.

The Unix operating system was at that time a bigger threat to IBM than even PC clones because these mid-sized systems threatened IBM's mainframe business and, more importantly, violated the closed software ecosystem IBM had worked so hard to create. Unix didn't come from IBM, for example. Sure there was, and still is, an IBM version of Unix called AIX, but, not surprisingly, it wasn't very good at the time. It is much better today. Attempts to get support for an AIX standard were not succeeding. This was before Open Source, but the mantra of Unix then was Open Standards, which meant multiple sources of interoperable software and lower costs. It hurt IBM's margins to compete with that.

Networking at IBM even into the 1990s meant mainly communicating with computer terminals—dumb IBM computer terminals at that—while the rest of the industry was quickly embracing intelligent terminals, microcomputers, and workstations generally connected by Xerox's local area network called Ethernet. IBM eventually responded to Ethernet with its own technology called Token Ring, but, in typical IBM fashion, it was lower in performance and higher in price.

Token Ring was rated at four megabits-per-second to Ethernet's 10 megabits. IBM touted the greater efficiency of its deterministic Token

Ring algorithm, but all Ethernet inventor Bob Metcalfe had to do was recite over and over again: "Ten is bigger than four." And though Token Ring was eventually souped-up to sixteen megabits, by that time Ethernet was going one hundred megabits—now a gigabit or more—and had already won the day. Corporate America was moving to networks in a big way and IBM was losing most of that business.

You've probably heard some of this before. But what many IBM followers have missed, however, was the impact of the merger of IBM's General Systems Division into the Data Processing Group starting in 1982. CEO John Opel pitched the merger as a better way of selling both PCs and typewriters along with mainframes, but it was really a kick in the head to both of the smaller platforms. Whatever focus IBM had on the low end of its business was hurt by this assertion of mainframe power. This gradual loss of focus grew over time, and by the early 1990s, with Akers in charge, the low end products were fatally damaged— damage that IBM inflicted entirely on itself.

Akers was clueless as to how to fix these problems. By 1993, IBM was a $40 billion company, facing a loss of more than $8 billion. To be fair, the plan Akers was trying to execute wasn't his, it was John Opel's. We'll see this again later in this story where another IBM CEO is put in peril by the strategic legacy of his predecessor.

IBM had to downsize, and quickly, or risk going under completely. Akers, who had spent his entire career at IBM—like every CEO before him except T.J. Watson, Sr.— appeared to be incapable of reconciling a hobbled IBM with the socially progressive employment practices under which more than 400,000 people had been hired. Suddenly IBM had 100,000 too many employees and a lifetime employment policy.

Since its founding in 1911 up until 1993, IBM had never laid off a single employee. Akers needed to, but somehow couldn't bring himself to do it. The company needed a hatchet man and John Akers was no hatchet man.

That was the old IBM, gone forever and never to return. It was the IBM of big ideas and big mistakes, too. Several of those mistakes led us to the current IBM, which was in large part created by the guy who was finally brought in by the IBM board to fix John Akers' (really John Opel's) mess -- Louis V. Gerstner, the first outsider ever to run Big Blue.

2

LOU GERSTNER SAVES
IBM FOR AWHILE

OUR IBM SALESMEN

(Sung to the tune, "Jingle Bells")

IBM, Happy men, smiling all the way.
Oh what fun it is to sell our products night and day.
IBM, Watson men, partners of T. J.
In his service to mankind – that's why we are so gay.

In the previous chapter I said IBM was more a country than a company, and that the country was a lot like Switzerland. The first time I made that analogy was in 1991 when it felt just right. But only two years later, in 1993, IBM was facing an $8 billion loss and near collapse, so maybe Switzerland wasn't such a good analogy after all. By 1993 IBM looked a lot more like early post-war Japan.

Let's take a moment here to consider what it would have meant had IBM collapsed in 1993. Most of its businesses would not have gone under; they would have gone into receivership. IBM would have been restructured in bankruptcy, drawn and quartered to some extent, but the profitable product lines would have survived. Mainly the company would have lost its traditional identity—it might no longer have even been called IBM—and it was this potential loss of identity, and loss of company culture, that was so crushing for everyone at IBM, from John Akers on down.

IBM had rich traditions, traditions that didn't emerge organically from the corporate structure but rather came from the personalities of the two Watsons who ran the company for the first 57 years. IBM was socially progressive, for example. That wasn't a prerequisite for success selling business machines or selling computers in the first half of the 20th century. It was the Watsonian ideal of how a modern company should be run:

IBM — A century of social responsibility

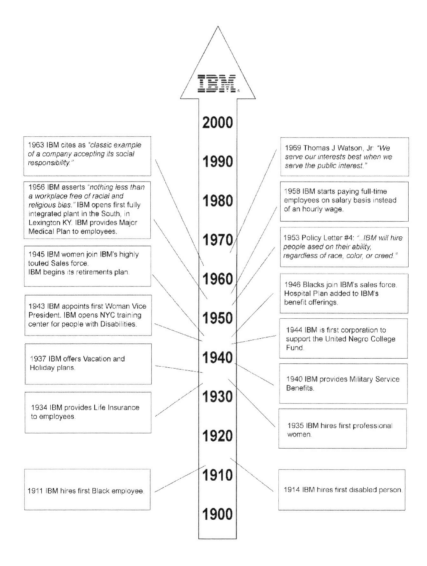

2000

1990
1963 IBM cites as *classic example of a company accepting its social responsibility.*

1969 Thomas J Watson, Jr: *"We serve our interests best when we serve the public interest."*

1980
1956 IBM asserts *"nothing less than a workplace free of racial and religious bias."* IBM opens first fully integrated plant in the South, in Lexington KY. IBM provides Major Medical Plan to employees.

1958 IBM starts paying full-time employees on salary basis instead of an hourly wage.

1970
1953 Policy Letter #4: *"...IBM will hire people ased on their ability, regardless of race, color, or creed."*

1945 IBM women join IBM's highly touted Sales force.
IBM begins its retirements plan.

1960
1946 Blacks join IBM's sales force. Hospital Plan added to IBM's benefit offerings.

1950
1943 IBM appoints first Woman Vice President. IBM opens NYC training center for people with Disabilities.

1944 IBM is first corporation to support the United Negro College Fund.

1940
1937 IBM offers Vacation and Holiday plans.

1940 IBM provides Military Service Benefits.

1930
1934 IBM provides Life Insurance to employees.

1920
1935 IBM hires first professional women.

1910
1911 IBM hires first Black employee.

1914 IBM hires first disabled person.

1900

Many lifelong IBM workers still with the company today feel betrayed by recent changes in this culture, which they tend to see as a compact between the corporation and its workers with "respect for the individual" as one of its mottos. But it wasn't a compact with IBM, it was a compact with the Watsons—a compact that survived on profitability, momentum, and nostalgia for 22 years after T.J. Watson, Jr. retired in 1971. The company kept Watson's compact for that long because doing so was within its means: IBM was so profitable in the 1970s that its cradle-to-grave benefit structure was easily affordable. But, by 1993, that financial cushion was gone, as were both the compact with the Watsons and the pretend compact with the IBM that succeeded them.

Thinking of IBM circa 1993 as similar to post-war or even feudal Japan is a useful exercise. IBM, for all its outward progressiveness, was and is a highly stratified society made of distinct classes. IBM has royalty, nobles, warriors, wizards, craftsmen, and serfs. Royalty for the longest time meant anyone with the last name Watson, but today it means the current CEO and nobody else. Nobility has always been conferred on managers who run core corporate functions like finance or human resources or entire business units. Warriors have always been in the sales department and nowhere else—this is key. Wizards are in research where they are misunderstood but respected. Craftsmen are journeymen programmers and engineers. Serfs are in manufacturing, customer service, and server administration.

The route to the CEO position at IBM has always been through the warrior class, through sales. A wizard can become management nobility but never the CEO. An old friend of mine and long retired IBMer did that, going from service technician to senior VP and business unit manager, but he was never in sales and so could never hope to be CEO, though I believe he deserved to be and the company would have been better for it.

If you read through the IBM official songbook, *Songs of the I.B.M.*, you'll see most of the songs were intended to be sung by salespeople (sales*men*) even if it was a song in praise of the head of IBM's patent office or of the "girls" (that's what they called them) in the steno pool. IBM had an army of outward-facing salespeople who defined the company to the world. The sales department, which can be seen as having let down the side in 1993, became particularly disillusioned by the company's troubles then, but as the warrior class they also took it upon themselves to fill any power vacuum wherever possible. They were quick to take advantage of the chaos that accompanied Akers' failure and replacement as CEO.

Homer Sarasohn, whom I mentioned in the Preface, as IBM's chief engineer in the era of the 650 and 801 mainframes right up to development of the 360 that really made the company a global success, was very familiar with what happened with a warrior class in a time of loss. As a young PhD from MIT, Sarasohn had been called to Japan by General Douglas MacArthur to rebuild Japan's electronics industry. Homer saw a humbled technocracy that was completely subservient to MacArthur and the Allied occupation, yet always learning, getting ready for a time when local power would be reasserted. That's what happened with the sales department at IBM.

While outwardly IBM was pulling together, inwardly the sales department felt singularly important because they brought in the money. The sales force didn't do the actual work of course, but then they never had. And with the breakdown of the Watsonian social compact, the sales department came to see itself as a class apart. They had their fingers on the pulse of the customer... or did they? Actually they had their fingers on the pulse of the head of IT, or worse still, the Chief Information Officer, who rarely knew what was actually happening in his or her company's own technology. So the sales department, IBM's supposed customer intelligence agency, was often listening to the wrong people, a mistake that went unnoticed for too long because the top levels of IBM were engaged primarily in denial.

The IBM sales department prepared for what became, and is to this day, internal class warfare.

Then along came Lou Gerstner, IBM's MacArthur.

Louis V. Gerstner, who took over running IBM from John F. Akers in 1993, wrote a book about his experiences there. *Who Says Elephants Can't Dance?* has many interesting stories and insights, but of course it only tells one side and certainly doesn't criticize Gerstner at all. My goal in this chapter is to put in the bits that Lou left out, to try and place his tenure in a more modern business context, and describe how he prepared IBM for its current difficulties.

To understand the difference between John Akers and Lou Gerstner, first look at their houses in Connecticut. This information is all easily available from public sources. According to Zillow.com, Akers' home in Westport, Conn. is worth $2.9 million—a nice place. Also according to Zillow, Gerstner's home in Greenwich, Conn. is worth $17.8 million—a *very* nice place. Both men are rich by most standards but Gerstner is a lot richer than Akers. That's an important data point.

Akers didn't work at IBM to get Big Rich, but Lou Gerstner did.

The former head of American Express and RJR Nabisco, Gerstner was brought in to save the company and he expected to be rewarded for doing so. His hiring set a new precedent for CEO compensation at IBM. Future IBM CEOs, whether they were hired from outside like Gerstner or came up through the ranks like all the others, would expect to be paid millions per year. This was a significant change in the way IBM was managed, and played a key role in the company's current problems, leading to even further social stratification.

A lot can be learned about companies by looking at their power and compensation structures. At companies where executive compensation is limited, power is generally measured by headcount—the total number of workers under a given executive. The more heads, the more power, which leads companies of that sort to be very inefficient in their labor practices. This described the old IBM of Akers and before.

Where executive salaries aren't especially limited, power often comes to be measured by the size of the paycheck, with CEO pay getting bigger and bigger for reasons that are rarely clear. IBM today has a split personality in this regard because top executives are paid well while lower executives and workers in general are paid below industry norms. So power at IBM is measured in dollars, except where it isn't. And where it isn't measured in dollars, power at IBM is still measured by headcount, which probably hurts the company.

Gerstner didn't respond to my request for an interview, but according to his book, the IBM he joined was both hierarchical and arrogant, with little direct communication across levels of the company and little need seen by top executives to explain, or even understand what was happening. The company was focused internally with little thought given to the actual needs of customers. Huge amounts of money were being spent to defeat Microsoft and Intel—battles already lost in Gerstner's view—while the mainframe business was being starved of funds and milked for profits by keeping prices artificially high.

To his credit, Gerstner changed these aspects of IBM culture while he was leading the company. Customers began to matter more, and IBM's headcount was reduced by 100,000. Gerstner acknowledged that Microsoft had effectively won the PC war. IBM started reinvesting in its near-monopoly mainframe business. All this was good.

Gerstner was able to make all these changes at what was previously perceived as an unchangeable company because he was hired with a mandate. Everyone, including IBM's customers, employees, and board members, expected Gerstner to make dramatic changes. He had to do that, and was allowed to do that to save the company. The alternative was oblivion and everyone knew that. In this respect Gerstner was MacArthur to IBM's Japan, and had it easy because he was given all the power. As an outsider he had no allegiance to the old IBM.

Every new CEO of a company enters with a mandate of sorts, but some mandates are stronger than others. Gerstner was empowered to do whatever it took to save IBM. Gerstner's successors didn't have as much freedom. Keep that in mind as we move forward.

The biggest change Gerstner made at IBM was shifting its focus, not just to the customer, but to selling services to that customer.

"The industry's disaggregation into thousands of niche players would make IT services a huge growth segment of the industry," Gerstner writes in his book. He was correct. IT services — managing computers, applications, and data for corporate and government customers — was not capital intensive like building new factories or even new products. It looked to Gerstner like easy money and IBM sure needed money. So Gerstner pushed IBM into the IT services business that is today the company's greatest source of profit.

As he attempted to transform IBM into a more responsive organization, Gerstner came up with some guiding principles that he listed in his book, specifically how they changed from the old IBM to the new. Here's the before and after of IBM as seen by Gerstner as CEO and presented in his book:

From	To
Product Out (I Tell You)	Customer In (in the shoes of the customer)
Do it my way	Do it the customer's way (provide real service)
Manage to morale	Manage to success
Decisions based on anecdotes and myths	Decisions based on facts and data
Relationship-driven	Performance-driven and measured
Conformity (politically correct)	Diversity of ideas and opinions

Attack the people	Attack the process (ask why, not who)
Looking good is equal to or more important than doing good	Accountability (always move the rocks)
United States (Armonk) dominance	Global sharing
Rule-drive	Principle driven
Value me (the silo)	Value us (the whole)
Analysis paralysis	Make decisions and move forward with urgency
Not invented here	Learning organization
Fund everything	Prioritize

Gerstner was an outsider but he wasn't totally ignorant of IBM, where his brother Dick Gerstner had long been a senior executive. Here's the brotherly advice Dick Gerstner gave to Lou before he started the new job:

- "Get an office and home PC. Use PROFS (the internal messaging system); your predecessor didn't and it showed.

- Publicly crucify shortsighted proposals, turf battles, and backstabbing. This may seem obvious, but these are an art form at IBM.

- Expect everything you say and do to be analyzed and interpreted, inside and outside the company.

- Find a private cadre of advisors who have no axes to grind.

- "Call your mom."

That's the end of my compliments for Lou Gerstner. The rest of this chapter is about mistakes he made at IBM. The first of these was the very way IBM went after the IT services business. Yes, Gerstner was customer-centric, but he wasn't living in the trenches, so the way the services business was conducted wasn't always the way he thought it was. Worse still, some bad decisions were made on Lou's watch, and they still reverberate today.

"Through the 1990s, IBM's biggest services accounts were Internal (meaning IBM itself), AT&T, and then others like Sears, Kodak, etc.," a longtime IBMer explained to me. "They didn't have a lot of accounts but the accounts were big. The Internal account was the biggest. It was IBM supporting itself. IBM had over 300,000 users, so this was a big account. IBM would often sell itself on what it was doing for itself. IBM wasn't a very demanding or even a very advanced, customer for its own services. Few file servers and LAN services existed, for example. Almost all documents were sent around as e-mail attachments. IBM's e-mail system was one of the most expensive on the planet. It cost IBM easily ten times more per user than comparable systems. IBM may also have sold its support services to itself at a profit—one division's profit was another division's cost."

Today, in 2014, there are still almost no corporate file servers at IBM. Employees still attach files to e-mails or upload them to a Notes application or a web application. The master customer database for IBM isn't a database at all. It's a spreadsheet. The company has an internal desktop back-up service; the only problem is it can take over *300 hours* to recover your data if you lose your hard drive. Three hundred hours is close to two weeks, during which time you can't get anything done.

The IBM Global Services division started in the spring of 1991, with the aim of helping companies manage their IT operations and resources. In the 1990s, most Global Services accounts were islands. The AT&T team worked autonomously and separately from the Sears team, and from the Kodak team, etc. Then, in an attempt to gain efficiency, IBM came up with the concept of the Geoplex, where they'd consolidate in one place local teams from a few accounts. There was some consolidation and cross-pollination of work and talent—that was the whole idea. Unfortunately it conflicted with the headcount-is-power ethos, so there was little incentive for one Geoplex to work with another. Each Geoplex tended to work autonomously from the others, and the IBM account teams worked with none of them.

During this time IBM could have been developing better techniques to support its accounts. Work was done on specific accounts, but never across Global Services. A technology team in Austin and the IBM internal account were driving all the decisions on tools and processes. The teams with the most experience in the subject—the ones that worked on the commercial accounts—were rarely involved in those efforts, and so what came out of Austin was not very useful.

Just as Gerstner was trying to expand Global Services in the 1990s, the division came under attack from competitors, including Electronic Data Systems (EDS) and Computer Sciences Corporation (CSC). These competitors offered customers simpler, clearer contracts. They were cheaper too. And IBM's competitors were especially successful with the smaller companies Big Blue didn't try very hard to win. This was because in the heart of the Gerstner era it still cost on average $600,000 for IBM just to sign a new services deal. The company couldn't make enough money from smaller accounts to cover the cost of signing them so they didn't bother.

"EDS would walk in and ask: How many desktops do you have?" recalled a former IBM Global Services sales engineer. "How many systems do you have? Here's your price. If your numbers were wrong, the price would be adjusted. The IBM way was to bring in a small army and spend months bidding the contract."

IBM, EDS, and CSC battled each other, driving down the price of services and trading customers throughout the 1990s. Then customers pushed cost cutting further by splitting their support services and having the firms bid separately on each part. You could walk into a business and find several vendors each doing part of the IT work and each of them refusing to work with the other. It was during this time that IBM began its move to find progressively cheaper, and cheaper, labor. First it sent work to Canada, then Brazil, and later to India. Despite Gerstner's bold talk, **at no time had IBM actually improved the quality, efficiency, or productivity of its services**. The business plan was to just throw cheaper bodies at it. This, of course, damaged quality, efficiency, and productivity. But that didn't matter to IBM since they could get eight Indian workers for the cost of one U.S. worker.

Much more on this offshoring later, but it began at IBM around 1997, five years before Gerstner's retirement.

Around 1997-1998, IBM Global Services reportedly made the decision that it was more profitable to cut back customer support and pay penalties when things broke, according to workers who were with that division then. That set in motion a new culture of cheating on accounts (more on this later). In the years that followed, IBM became increasingly emboldened to do less and cut corners more on its accounts. Again, this was on Gerstner's watch. He probably didn't even know it was happening.

Since data is the lifeblood of all big businesses, when IT is done well companies usually do well. When IT is done poorly, however, customers often find themselves in trouble a few years later. As information systems are neglected, management becomes less effective. While IBM may have contributed to the demise of some of its customers, this was part of a much bigger industry trend. Many companies worked hard at going cheap on IT, and they eventually took a beating for it. Names like Sears, Sprint, BestBuy, and, more recently, Target, come to mind.

What happened to: "Dedication to every client's success?"

The second-biggest mistake made at IBM by Lou Gerstner was selling the company's networking division to AT&T at the end of 1998. But, according to Gerstner, the sale was quite a coup. He writes:

"What did occur to me was that we had an asset that most of these (networking) companies would be seeking to build over the next five years. And if the world was moving in the direction we anticipated — toward a glut of many networks — then the value of our network would never be higher. So we chose to auction it off to the highest bidder. We thought we'd be doing well to get $3.5 billion. But the frenzy eventually produced a bid of $5 billion from AT&T; that was an extraordinary price for a business that produced a relatively tiny percentage of IBM's profit."

The real story of the networking sale is more complex. There were many reasons why IBM might have wanted to sell the division. For one, it was a way of eliminating 5,000 positions without severance benefits, transferring those employees and their future benefits to AT&T as part of the deal. And IBM's networking division, like the rest of IBM's IT services, had as its biggest customer IBM itself. IBM networking was by far the most expensive supplier, so offloading it should have cut costs internally — costs that may have been overly inflated by internal rivalries now gone. These perfectly good reasons for selling appeared to be compounded by the emerging sense in the late 1990s that networks were becoming commodities, bought and sold by the pound. What was the difference if the supplier was IBM, MCI, AT&T, or Global Crossing? Bits were bits. So the deal was done.

And IBM has been regretting it internally ever since.

AT&T may have been willing to pay more than any other bidder for IBM's network, but that didn't mean AT&T was the best networking vendor of those companies that bid. And this wasn't a simple matter of selling off an asset that could be replaced overnight, because AT&T, for its high price, expected to retain IBM's business for years to come. That was part of the deal.

Former IBM workers now working at AT&T hadn't been well managed in the first place, and were now further confounded by AT&T management that had a traditional phone company (regulated monopoly) attitude toward customer service, which wasn't good. IBM had given up control of the networking aspect of not only its own business but also the business of those Global Services customers whose networking needs had been served directly by IBM. Those companies were now customers of a customer of a phone company. Service suffered and still does, 15 years later.

Gerstner seriously injured his company by auctioning the network business to the highest bidder. He probably should have sold it, but to a lower bidder that was a better networking vendor than AT&T.

But the biggest mistake made by Lou Gerstner as CEO of IBM probably was hiring Sam Palmisano as his successor. Here's what Gerstner said about that in his book:

"...I was an outsider. But that was my job. I know Sam Palmisano has an opportunity to make the connections to the past as I could never do. His challenge will be to make them without going backward; to know that the centrifugal forces that drove IBM to be inward-looking and self-absorbed still lie powerful in the company."

3

SAM PALMISANO AND
THE LONG CON

Despite his stumbles, Lou Gerstner both saved IBM and transformed it.

We now know the scene was more complex than presented in the press at the time, but Gerstner has to be credited with saving the company, and handing it in 2002 to Sam Palmisano in far better shape than when Gerstner had joined IBM in 1993. While Palmisano still had to make decisions and lead the company, his greatest challenge at IBM was simply to not screw it up. If it ain't broke, don't fix it. Well Palmisano fixed IBM anyway, and today it is broken as a result.

That's not what the press said when Palmisano retired on the last day of 2011, handing the top job to Ginni Rometty, but this just emphasizes how difficult it is to know what's really happening inside enormous companies. When things go wrong it can take years, or even decades, for the true impact to be clear. And in an era when the typical Fortune 500 CEO is on the job for only about four years, making changes that show short-term benefits, despite associated long-term problems, can be very tempting indeed.

One legacy Sam Palmisano gleefully accepted from Lou Gerstner was the former CEO's level of compensation. Palmisano's bonus was based on how IBM performed on Wall Street, so that performance came to guide IBM completely during Palmisano's tenure. And he was great at producing those numbers, as a result retiring with a package valued at $271 million, according to footnoted.com. This was among the most expensive American CEO retirements at that time, and far more than Gerstner got for saving the company.

But to look at press accounts of the time, Palmisano was worth every cent.

"I.B.M.'s profits have increased sharply since Mr. Palmisano took over, and its stock price climbed," noted the New York Times. "Earlier this year, IBM passed Microsoft to become the second most valuable technology company, measured by market capitalization, trailing only Apple, the consumer technology powerhouse."

Here is how Fortune described Palmisano's legacy: "Nine years after Gerstner stepped down as CEO, IBM is financially and strategically stronger and, yes, sexier than ever — all thanks to Sam Palmisano, Gerstner's successor. Under Palmisano, earnings have quadrupled and the stock is up 57 percent. He's not merely cutting costs (though he's done plenty of that, including shifting work from the US to India). He's remaking the company by pushing into new countries and expanding hot businesses, such as supercomputing and analytics that require heavy-duty lab innovations."

Academics, too, approved of Palmisano's strategy at IBM. The Harvard Business Review went so far as to rave: "In the 20th century, a select group of leaders, including General Motor's Alfred Sloan, Hewlett-Packard's David Packard and Bill Hewlett, and GE's Jack Welch, set the standard for the way corporations are run. In the 21st century only IBM's Sam Palmisano has done so."

But wait, there's more! Here's how the Review summed-up Palmisano's IBM career: "They don't give Nobel Prizes in management, but if they did, Sam Palmisano would deserve one."

Harvard Professor Bill George's analysis of the job Palmisano did at IBM, which he characterized as five important steps, certainly characterize to some extent what happened at IBM in the Palmisano years, but I'd call it mainly a *mischaracterization*. The first step, according to George, was to "craft the strategy and organization to implement the vision."

But what was Palmisano's vision? Gerstner had already downsized, cut fat, jettisoned what he could of the Watsonian compact with IBM employees, and moved the company into services. It wasn't clear to anyone at the time how Palmisano would be anything but

another Gerstner, though this time with the advantage (advantage?) of having spent his whole career at IBM.

Palmisano's first act, as Professor George explains, was to dissolve the Corporate Executive Council on which the 11 top executives of IBM sat to vote on policies. Dumping the CEC consolidated power in the office of the CEO once Gerstner's token year as chairman was over, Palmisano was then president, CEO, and chairman, and had unfettered control of IBM with essentially no checks and balances in place. It was an opportunity for bold action, indeed a chance to transcend even Gerstner. Further, it would represent the final victory of sales over the rest of IBM. Now — what to do with all that power?

Palmisano found his windfall in the simple expedient of "maximizing shareholder value."

Lawyers arguing in court present legal theories — their ideas of how the world and the law intersect, and why this should mean their client is right and the other side is wrong. Proof of one legal theory over another comes in the form of a verdict or court decision. As a culture we have many theories about institutions and behaviors that aren't so clear-cut in their validity tests (no courtroom, no jury) yet we cling to these theories to feel better about the ways we have chosen to live our lives. In American business, especially, one key theory is that the purpose of corporate enterprise is to "maximize shareholder value." Some take this even further and claim that **such maximization is the *only* reason a corporation exists**. Watch CNBC or Fox Business News long enough and you'll begin to believe this is the God's truth, but it's not. It's just a theory.

It's not even a very old theory, in fact, and only dates back to 1976. That's when Michael Jensen and William Meckling of the University of Rochester published a paper, "Theory of the Firm: Managerial Behavior, Agency Costs and Ownership Structure" in *The Journal of Financial Economics*. Their theory, in a nutshell, was that there was an inherent conflict in business between owners (shareholders) and managers, and that this conflict had to be resolved in favor of the owners, who after all *owned* the business; and the best way to do that was to find a way to align those interests by linking managerial compensation to owner success. Link executive compensation primarily to the stock price, the economists argued, and this terrible conflict would be resolved, making business somehow, well, better.

This idea appears to be more of a solution in search of a problem. If the CEO is driving the company into bankruptcy or spends too much money on his own perks, for example, the previous theory of business (and the company bylaws) said shareholders could vote the bum out. But that's so mundane, so imprecise for economists who see a chance to elegantly align interests and make the system work smoothly and automatically. The only problem is the alignment of interests suggested by Jensen and Meckling works just as well — maybe even better — if management just cooks the books and lies. And so shareholder value maximization gave us companies like Enron (Jeffrey Skilling in prison), Tyco International (Dennis Kozlowski in prison), and WorldCom (Bernie Ebbers in prison).

It's just a theory, remember.

The Jensen and Meckling paper shook the corporate world because it presented a reason to pay executives more — a lot more — if they made the stock rise. Not if they made a better product, cured a disease, or helped defeat a national enemy. All they had to do was make the stock go up. Through the 1960s and 1970s, average CEO compensation in America per dollar of corporate earnings had gone down 33 percent as companies became more efficient at making money. But now there was a (dubious) reason for compensation to go up, up, up, which it has done consistently for almost 40 years, until now when we think this is the way the corporate world is supposed to work — even its *raison d'être*.

But in that same time real corporate performance has gone down. The average rate of return on invested capital for public companies in the United States is a quarter of what it was in 1965. Sure, productivity has gone up, but that can be done through automation or by beating more work out of employees (more on that later).

Jensen and Meckling created the very problem they purported to solve — a problem that really hadn't existed in the first place.

Maximizing shareholder return dropped the compounded rate of return on the S&P 500 from 7.5 percent annually from 1933-76, to 6.5 percent annually from 1977 to today. That one percent may not look like much, but from the point of view of the lady at the bank the loss of so much compound interest may well have led to our corporate malaise of today. Profits are high — but are they real? Stocks are high — but few investors, managers, or workers are really happy or secure.

Maximizing shareholder return is bad policy both for public companies and for our society in general. That's what Jack Welch told the Financial Times in 2009, once Welch was safely out of the day-to-day earnings grind at General Electric: "On the face of it," said Welch, "shareholder value is the dumbest idea in the world. Shareholder value is a result, not a strategy... your main constituencies are your employees, your customers, and your products. Managers and investors should not set share-price increases as their overarching goal. ... Short-term profits should be allied with an increase in the long-term value of a company."

Tell that to Sam Palmisano at IBM, who, in 2005, and then again in 2010, set corporate goals for earnings-per-share, which is to say he set a target price for IBM stock based on historical price-to-earnings ratios, as one of his signature goals for the company. And he was applauded for it.

"...the dumbest idea in the world," Jack Welch said. Remember that.

I didn't come up with this idea that shareholder earnings maximization should not be the prime corporate motivator. It came from Roger Martin, former dean of the Rotman School of Management at the University of Toronto, only 169 miles from Rochester where this nonsense began. Martin's very good book is *Fixing the Game: Bubbles, Crashes, and What Capitalism Can Learn from the NFL*. Here's how Martin put it: "Imagine an NFL coach holding a press conference on Wednesday to announce that he predicts a win by nine points on Sunday, and that bettors should recognize that the current spread of six points is too low. Or picture the team's quarterback standing up in the post-game press conference and apologizing for having only won by three points when the final betting spread was nine points in his team's favor. While it's laughable to imagine coaches or quarterbacks doing so, CEOs are expected to do both of these things."

Martin contrasts two markets he calls the real market and the expectations market. The real market is where goods and services are produced, bought and sold, which is to say the real world in which most of us live. The expectations market predicts a certain performance and then delivers on it through whatever means necessary. **The expectations market is really just gambling.**

Sam Palmisano placed the largest earnings bet in U.S. corporate history when in 2010 he projected IBM would post earnings per share of $20 in 2015.

Consider the audacity of what Palmisano did. He not only tied the very existence of IBM to reaching an earnings goal five years in the future, but he did so knowing that it wasn't even on his watch that success or failure would be measured. He saddled the new CEO Ginni Rometty with that.

No other U.S. company predicts corporate earnings five years out because no other U.S. corporation is willing to assume that much risk. Companies give guidance—their best guess—to analysts a quarter or two in advance. But to predict with any assurance what earnings will be 20 quarters from now is probably impossible because there is no way of even knowing what a company's mix of successful products and services will be by that time. Yet Sam Palmisano did it anyway, possibly as an act of faith in IBM.

Or maybe it was the long con. You decide.

The "long or big con, is a scam that unfolds over several days or weeks and involves a team of swindlers, as well as props, sets, extras, costumes, and scripted lines. It aims to rob the victim of thousands of dollars, often by getting him or her to empty out banking accounts and borrow from family members," according to Wikipedia.

By predicting earnings five years out, Palmisano effectively damped out quarterly earnings issues for IBM. Big Blue had more than reached its first five-year target of $10 per share by 2010, despite the worst recession in 70 years. Who then would bet that Palmisano couldn't do it again?

Bernie Ebbers, Dennis Kozlowski, Bernie Madoff, and Jeff Skilling all played versions of the long con. But maybe Sam Palmisano was different. Maybe Sam could actually do it. It is my opinion that at the beginning of his tenure, Palmisano believed that himself, trusting in the ingenuity and loyalty of the people of IBM.

Remember IBM is a feudal culture where the sales organization is dominant. What matters to the IBM salesman are the parts of the company above him because he yearns for an eventual role in management—IBM nobility. She thrills to the idea of someday becoming IBM's CEO. Beneath that salesperson lies the rest of IBM, comprising about 350,000 workers who are completely expendable. They are resources, their only purpose being to create something new to sell, and then to deliver it. And if they can't deliver it, well then, they deserve to die. That's the ethos.

Analysts can argue whether IBM will make its $20 target or not, but they haven't bothered to make another obvious calculation: What

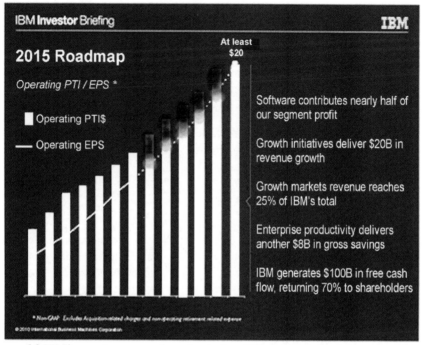

would IBM's earnings per share be today if Palmisano had done nothing at all? I think earnings would already be higher than $20 per share, which makes me wonder what Sam — and now Ginni — have been up to all along?

Knowing what we know now, Sam Palmisano's success as CEO of IBM so far can be attributed almost entirely to luck.

Here's the important part, some of it repeated from before for emphasis:

IBM is a sales company, run by salespeople. They are the Japanese warriors.

With the exception of the one-time "outsider" hire of Gerstner, IBM salespeople are the only people who can become CEO or make it to the executive ranks of the company. They are generally lifers. This means they have **no outside IBM experience**. They see the world in an IBM-only way.

Outside hires have a broader worldview and their tendency to react to IBM's internal weird ways of doing things is quickly spotted. Their outside view is considered a fault and is not respected.

When a deal is lost or sales are not up to par, in IBM's culture someone has to be blamed and often punished. A sales rep can be given a poor rating and then put through a managed "improvement plan." If the sale of a specific product is lost, the people who represented it can be punished. The sales organization often blames other IBM teams for their failures.

With Services revenue now dropping, with Systems sales dropping, with overall net income dropping — it has to be **someone's fault.** It is IBM's culture to punish. The layoffs, the frozen pay, the furloughs — all of it are IBM's way of saying you have failed the sales organization. Sales are the only important thing in IBM and everything else is secondary. If customers are not buying, it has to be someone's fault. Punishing people is the way IBM fixes its problems.

Because IBM's leadership has **no outside world experience,** punishing people is the only solution to their problems. They do not understand the business process or the fact that management might need improvement. They do not understand that investments in improvements are periodically needed to insure the health and effectiveness of every operation.

Since Palmisano started setting public earnings targets in the investment community, IBM's new customer is Wall Street. Sam sold Wall Street on $20 earnings-per-share and an increasing stock price as a result. IBM's leadership today is singularly focused on continuing this plan. If the EPS and financial numbers are not met, and if the stock price doesn't continue to rise; it has to be someone in IBM's fault. That's the conventional wisdom.

What Sam Palmisano and his executive team (and the Harvard Business Review) missed was the outside world, and what was happening when IBM's stock began to soar in 2007. It wasn't because of anything special that IBM was doing. It was circumstantial. It was luck. When the financial system and stock market tanked, IBM was one of the few large, financially stable companies with an international sales base. IBM suddenly became a "safe" investment.

Lou Gerstner had already fixed IBM's businesses. Most of IBM's business is done through multi-year contracts. Even if IBM had a really bad year, its financials might only take a slight hit. Those multi-year contracts tended to average out the bad times.

Sam could have done nothing and his tenure at CEO would have been considered exemplary. A decade ago, the banking industry was trying hard to become the darling of Wall Street. Banks' earnings statements were soaring. Their stocks were soaring. What we didn't know in 2004 was what amazing reckless and stupid things the banks were doing to make money. It took the Great Recession of 2008 and a huge banking bailout to show how rotten that industry was. How is IBM any different today? It isn't.

IBM wasn't the only company to embrace maximizing shareholder return. Heck, most of them do it, though to a lesser extent. But IBM, through its five-year earnings plans, has embraced the expectations market more clearly than any other big U.S. industrial company. IBM will do anything—anything—to reach its 2015 earnings goal of $20 per share, even if it means destroying the company, even if it means hurting customers.

Peter Drucker, who had been writing about business for 50 years before Jensen and Meckling wrote their paper in 1976, said the only purpose of a business was "to create a customer." The chapters to come will show in great detail what a lousy job IBM has been doing at that lately.

4

WHY BIG COMPANIES CAN'T CHANGE

There's a very good TED Talk (Technology, Entertainment, Design; a global set of conferences owned by the private, non-profit Sapling Foundation) by leadership expert and author Simon Sinek about how great leaders inspire their companies by asking "Why?" I think it also goes a long way toward explaining why big companies don't handle change well. It's not that they can't ask "Why?" It's that the answer doesn't make sense at their scale, though it should.

The Dow 30 Industrials that make up that all-important stock average began in 1896 as the Dow 12; and of those original 12 only General Electric survives on the list today. None of the other 11 is on today's list even under different names, though some of the companies do survive. Many of those former industry titans, companies like American Tobacco and U.S. Leather, no longer exist at all. In some ways that's surprising since big industrial companies take decades to build, and since we continue to need most of the stuff they make—what was the problem?

Times change and big companies don't like to change with the times.

At the polar opposite position from big industrial companies sit startups, nearly every one of which begins with an effortless expression of "Why?" Big companies ask "What?" and then "How?" but almost never "Why?" according to Sinek, who I think has it absolutely right. But good startups are motivated from birth by "Why?"

That "Why?" is traditionally quite simple: because the founders want one for themselves. A hardware device or software application doesn't exist and they'd really like one, so they invent it. For startups "Why?" is easy. If it isn't easy to answer the question then you probably don't have a good startup.

If a founder's answer to "Why?" is "to get rich" they are in the wrong job, because wealth is almost always a byproduct of good work, not its objective.

If we apply this idea to a more mature company, like Apple, we can see the "Why" of the iPod and iTunes was "to take your entire music collection with you wherever you go." That sort of thinking isn't common in big companies. Some of this is due to scale, some due to arrogance, and some to having simply lost their way. But no matter how big a company grows, asking "Why?" is still vital for continued success. They just don't know it.

Even at Microsoft, in the 1980s and 1990s, the answer was clear and understood down to every employee: "To put a computer running Microsoft software on every desk and in every home." But that was then, and I bet if you asked the same question at Microsoft today you'd get many different answers, which shows the trouble *that* company is in.

Back in 1986, I helped write the business plan for Illustrator, Adobe Systems' first consumer product. The "Why?" for Illustrator was "Because Adobe founder John Warnock wants a drawing program." As I recall, the business plan had the new consumer division with a net-net positive cash position of $87,000 after five years. Millions invested creating an entire new business for a new set of customers through a completely new distribution channel for a lousy $87,000?

Most mature companies would never have done it.

Yet if you look at Adobe's market cap this morning—just under $34 billion—probably $33 billion of that is based on consumer and professional software that began with Illustrator. That $87,000 grew to $33 billion over 28 years.

Adobe had an OEM cash cow business selling printer controller designs and software in 1986, but that could only grow so big. Thanks primarily to Microsoft, who cloned Adobe's PostScript, that OEM business eventually declined. PostScript is only a small part of Adobe today.

This sounds to me like the position faced by many large, successful companies with mature product lines that were facing obvious challenges down the road. Such companies (I'm sure you can name a bunch if you think about it) see the problem approaching, but are paralyzed by the need to envision $10 billion replacement markets. They can't do what Adobe did in 1986 because there is no obvious answer to "Why?", and a proposal to make $87,000 after five years wouldn't even get in front of the board for approval, no matter how important it really was to the company's survival.

Adobe was lucky to have a curious founder still at the helm. It was lucky to be making enough money to risk a few million on an alternate future too.

But 2014 is nothing like 1986. Looking five years ahead for business justification isn't done any more. Heck, five *quarters* is a long time in business today. But then the average CEO tenure is also, what, four years?

And that's why big successful companies tend to roll over and die.

Why IBM Can't Change:

What is IBM's current answer to the question "Why?"? They don't have an answer. They haven't had one for decades.

What would Steve Jobs say about IBM? Steve was hardly an ideal boss himself, but there's no denying he knew how to effect corporate change in a way that kept Apple ahead of market trends and grew the company's market cap by more than 500 times (50,000 percent!) during his tenure as CEO. I spoke with Steve about IBM in my film *Steve Jobs: The Lost Interview* and he put it in a very useful context for this chapter:

"If you were a product person at IBM or Xerox—so you make a better copier or a better computer, so what? When you have a monopoly market share the company is not any more successful. So the people who can make the company more successful are in sales and marketing and they end up running the companies. And the product people get driven out of decision-making forums. And the companies forget what it means to make great products. Sort of the product sensibility and the product genius that brought them to that monopolistic position gets rotted out by people running these companies who have no conception of a good product versus a bad product... They really have no feeling in their hearts usually about wanting to help customers."

This is the first thing to understand about the IBM of today: The company is being run by executives who, for the most part, don't understand the products and services they sell. The IBM of today is a sales organization. There is nothing wrong with sales if you can also deliver, but increasingly IBM can't deliver.

Jobs also explains why IBM can't deliver well. It's IBM's maniacal fixation on process — once a strength, but now a cancer:

"...big companies get confused. When they start getting bigger they want to replicate their initial success. And a lot of them think, well, somehow there is some magic in the process of how that success was created, so they start to institutionalize process across the company. And before very long people get confused that the process is the content. And that's ultimately the downfall of IBM. IBM has the best process people in the world. They just forgot about the content."

Steve Jobs had this exactly right when he said this *in 1995*, just two years after Gerstner came aboard to save IBM.

The IPod and ITunes marked a Apple's business started by people throughout Apple asking questions like "Why?" Apple was selling lots of iMac's with CD burners. Why? People were ripping a lot of music. They were creating mixes of music, burning them on CDs for their personal CD players. Back in the 1990s portable music players were modestly popular items (especially the SONY Walkman) but they didn't work very well. By asking a lot of questions Apple came up with the idea of the IPod and ITunes, a success that altered forever three industries — music, consumer electronics, and computers.

Asking questions starts an important process in a business. It gets people to talk. It gets them to share ideas. It leads to brainstorming. When the collective intelligence of the employees of a company is focused on a problem or an idea, powerful things can happen.

This has not happened in IBM for years.

In the years that followed my video interview with Steve Jobs in 1995, IBM's Global Services division became the cash engine of the corporation. But when other companies got into the IT outsourcing business IBM began to face serious competition. For a few years IBM resisted change, and tried to sell the IBM name and reputation. In a competitive market PRICE SELLS. In a competitive market price is more important than name and reputation.

IBM, being a sales company, started lowering their price. The problem is they forgot the content. No provision was made to deliver the same service better and cheaper. IBM cut corners and reduced the quality of its service.

In situations like this companies that know how to change start asking questions. They start talking. They start brainstorming. They start finding ways to change. IBM didn't.

IBM's idea of change in Global Services started with making its employees work excessive amounts of unpaid overtime.

A few years ago, just over 32,000 IBM server administrators (about 10 percent of the company at the time) were being forced to work overtime without extra pay. IBM lost a class action lawsuit and paid a $65 million settlement. That's about $2,000 per affected employee before the lawyers took their share. Then IBM gave all those disaffected workers a 15 percent pay cut with the justification they'd more than get it back in their new overtime pay. Then IBM restricted the workers to 40-hour weeks so there would be no overtime pay.

VP approval was required each time someone was needed to work overtime. The net result was that all the server admins worked exactly 40 hours per week, and for 15 percent less pay. I'm told by some of those IBMers involved that they were then put at the top of the next layoff list and eventually let go. At the end of their severance pay period after being laid off, many were rehired as contractors for less money and no benefits. At that point they were at 50-60 percent of their original pay. Eventually most of those jobs were shipped overseas after the American workers were, in many cases, forced to train their foreign replacements.

This story has a *Bridge on the River Kwai* feel to it, don't you think?

That movie ends with the destruction of the bridge they worked so hard to build. The same thing is happening to IBM's existing businesses today. Over the years the quality of IBM's service suffered, and IBM's customers suffered. It has become increasingly difficult for IBM to retain customers and sign new business. Contracts have been canceled prematurely, settlements have been paid, and there have been lawsuits. IBM's iconic name and reputation is under attack, from IBM's own actions!

All products, services, and businesses change over time. Change is an important and necessary part of most successful companies. Change is a process that starts with asking questions.

In IBM's Global Services business they should have been constantly asking questions. Questions like, "Why are we in business?

How can we do our work better, faster, cheaper? What is the competition doing? How can we serve our customers better?"

This has never happened in services at IBM. In Global Services, the contract was the gospel, it was the law. Any idea or suggestion to do things better or differently was immediately dismissed because "it was not in the contract." Worse, IBM is a very feudal organization. The serfs are never supposed to be seen or heard. Only the privileged few are allowed to think. IBM invested heavily in pet projects that either didn't work or provided no improvements for the services business. The big idea to improve the business was to replace their old serfs with new serfs who were cheaper, less educated, and less experienced.

In 1981, IBM thought it would sell 250,000 units of its new PC. Did it know it would grow into a multi-billion-dollar industry?

In 1992, did IBM know the first smartphone, its own Simon, was the harbinger of a multi-billion dollar industry?

In 2001, did Apple know its IPod would grow into a multi-billion-dollar business?

Multi-billion-dollar business ideas are exceedingly rare. Everyone hopes that their idea will grow into a multi-billion-dollar business. Virtually no one knows if a business idea has that potential.

Why was Apple successful, while IBM was not? This is a critical question because it gives an indication of future success or failure in IBM.

Most multi-billion-dollar businesses are a result of years of evolution, years of constant investment, years of change and improvement. Throughout the business, questions are being asked, ideas are being discussed — the whole organization is thinking!

In the PC industry, IBM lost its leadership position when it tried to control the industry. The more it tried to exert control, the more control it lost. This was a classic case of a company not listening.

IBM's smart phone was years ahead of its time. It was a great idea, and something IBM should have continued to research and develop. When the technology and market were ready, IBM could have been a major player in a huge new business.

But IBM does not want to be a commodity, mass producer of anything. They couldn't become a low-cost, high-volume maker of PCs, so they eventually sold the business to Lenovo Group Ltd., now headquartered in China and North Carolina.

The thought of making millions of consumer electronic smart phones is probably terrifying to IBM. They do not have the culture to engineer a highly integrated device that can be mass-produced inexpensively.

Most products and services evolve into a commodity and operate in a competitive market. This is part of the classic business lifecycle. IBM, being a sales company, tends to exit a business when the selling gets tough. Being a sales company, IBM does not know it needs to continuously improve its products and services so that when competition gets tougher it is still easy to sell.

Apple is successful today because it was open to new ideas. It pursued a few new good ideas, and over the years it constantly invested in and improved those ideas.

If IBM can't change and recover its lost youth, and if management as re-instituted by Palmisano post-Gerstner has no sense of product, just process, and they are deliberately divorced even from the process part (Palmisano added several layers of management between his office and the reality of IBM) then what's left to do?

Well, they are salesmen, aren't they, these top leaders of IBM? So they sell.

Today IBM is always trying to find and buy new $10 billion businesses. Anything they sell has to be big to have the proper impact on earnings-per-share, so no small ideas are allowed. Nor are cheap ideas allowed, either, because in this expectations market where the real IBM customer is Wall Street, not corporate America, the sizzle is just as important as the steak. So IBM needs $10 billion ideas that cost at least $1 billion each because $1 billion is a nice big number that shows resolve and might even hint of brilliance.

If only it were so.

5

LEAN AND MEAN

I wrote extensively in 2007 about management problems at IBM Global Services, explaining how the executive ranks from then-CEO Sam Palmisano on down were losing touch with reality. They were bidding contracts too low to make a profit, and then mismanaging them in an attempt to make a profit anyway, often to the detriment of IBM customers. Those columns and the reaction they created within the ranks at IBM showed just how bad things had become.

Then they got worse.

That was according to my many friends at Big Blue who believed they were about to undergo the biggest restructuring of IBM since the Gerstner days, only this time for all the wrong reasons.

The IBM restructuring project was called LEAN, and the first manifestation of LEAN was 1,300 layoffs at various Global Services Centers in early May, 2007, which generated almost no press. Thirteen hundred layoffs from a company with more than 350,000 workers is nothing, so the yawning press reaction was not unexpected. But that *resource action*, as they refer to it inside IBM management, was a rehearsal for what I understood were tens of thousands of layoffs to follow, each dribbled out until some reporter (that would be me) noticed the growing trend. Then IBM would dump people *en masse* when the jig was up, but no later than the end of 2007.

Decisions about who to fire reportedly had been made; senior managers had been under orders to keep the news from their affected employees. I suggested at the time that if you worked at IBM Global Services, you should have asked your boss outright if you were on the list to be fired. It would have put the boss in a bind, sure, but might have led to a sort of *Alice's Restaurant* effect in which hypocrisy was confronted and exposed.

The Toyota Production System — more magical thinking:

IBM's LEAN was supposed to have been based on another program called Lean (not LEAN) that characterized the Toyota Production System (TPS) — Toyota Motors' answer to Henry Ford's method of mass production. Academics from MIT had studied how Toyota became such a successful car company and discovered TPS, which they relabeled *Lean Manufacturing*, and described to the world. Lean was Toyota's approach to almost every aspect of its business with the idea of continual quality improvement through the refinement of process. Remember, IBM *loved* process, so the idea of Lean was very compelling. And there was good reason to believe it could be successfully applied to services, and even to the development of software. But, as had become the IBM way, they interpreted Lean differently. They corrupted it to their own ends.

IBM initially called its program LEAN, though apparently that's not an acronym. Later the name was changed to Lean, presumably to be more like Toyota, but to differentiate between the two I will call IBM's program LEAN, and Toyota's will be Lean.

In their book, *The Machine that Changed the World,* James Womack, Daniel Roos, and Daniel Jones distilled Toyota's Lean down to five principles:

1) Specify the value desired by the customer.

2) Identify the value stream for each product, provide that value, and challenge all of the wasted steps (generally nine out of 10) currently necessary to provide it.

3) Make the product flow continuously through the remaining value-added steps.

4) Introduce pull between all steps where continuous flow is possible. (Pull is communication between steps to help them proceed synchronously.)

5) Manage toward perfection, so that the number of steps and

the amount of time and information needed to serve the customer continually falls.

Notice that not one of those steps says "Lay off thousands of workers."

"What IBM is doing isn't Lean at all," explained Mark Graban, a recognized expert in Lean methodology for service industries like health care and IT. "In fact, Lean as practiced by Toyota, began with a vow by management that no jobs will be eliminated because a successful company will always need more good workers. Duties might change but there would be no layoffs."

IBM sent representatives to Lean classes and later held classes of their own, but what was apparently picked up by the top managers in Armonk was a Cliff Notes version of Lean that said it was a great excuse for eliminating workers. In fact, in one IBM Town Hall meeting, an IBM VP referred to LEAN as "a veiled attempt to eliminate U.S.A. jobs," which of course it was.

IBM's LEAN was about offshoring and outsourcing at a rate never seen before at IBM. Big Blue had been ramping up its operations in India and China with what I was told was the ultimate goal of laying off one American worker for each overseas hire. The big plan was to continue until at least half of Global Services had been cut from the U.S. division. LEAN meetings were quite specifically aimed at identifying common and repetitive work that could be automated or moved offshore, and finding work Global Services was doing that it should not have been doing at all. The idea was that once extraneous work was eliminated, it would be easier to move the rest offshore.

All this was to have happened by the end of 2007, at which point IBM planned to freeze its U.S. pension plan.

Inherent in Toyota's version of Lean was a vital feedback loop between labor and management to identify places where efficiencies could be gained and products improved. IBM's LEAN system in action had no such feedback loop, with all job cuts coming from the top with little to no input from the people actually doing the work or, indeed, from their managers. The rationalization for such an approach was two-fold:

1) It was more efficient (and ruthless) to do it this way.

2) It didn't matter anyway because at IBM the belief was that bodies could be freely substituted, one for another, with no loss of efficiency. A programmer in India or Argentina was

the exact functional equivalent of a programmer in the U.S.A.

The point of IBM's LEAN had nothing to do with the work itself and had everything to do with the price of IBM shares. Remove at least 100,000 heads, eliminate the long-term drag of a defined-benefit pension plan, and the price of IBM stock would soar. This is exactly the kind of story Wall Street loved to hear. Palmisano and his lieutenants would retire rich!

And not long after that, my sources at IBM predicted, IBM's business would crash.

IBMers told me of a broad expectation at all levels of IBM familiar with the LEAN plan that it was going to cause huge problems for the company. Even the executives who supported this campaign most strongly expected it to go down poorly with employees and customers alike because service would suffer and no customer money would be saved. But in the end IBM management did it anyway, which showed that only the reaction of Wall Street mattered anymore.

So we expected round after round of layoffs, muted a bit, as they were back in the Gerstner days by some of those same people being hired back as consultants at 75 percent of their former pay and 50 percent of their former cost to the company since they wouldn't be getting benefits. Throw in some overtime and it wouldn't look bad on paper for the people, but it was also very temporary.

If you took a purely business school approach to this news back then, it probably wouldn't have looked so bad for IBM. What was wrong with a multinational corporation moving work to its own overseas divisions? If you squinted hard enough, it might have looked like good management. Global Services was overweight and inefficient. Something had to be done and the company had already considered (and apparently rejected) a range of options, right up to putting Global Services on the auction block.

The problem with LEAN was that offshoring on this scale created huge communications and logistical problems, didn't improve customer relations, and wouldn't have saved money for years without the parallel gutting of the pension plan.

And it was just plain mean.

It was especially disconcerting for an action of this scale to have taken place at a time when many tech companies (including IBM) were complaining about a shortage of technical workers to justify a proposed expansion of H-1B and other guest worker visa programs. (The **H-1B** is a non-immigrant visa that allows U.S. employers to temporarily employ foreign workers in specialty occupations.) What was wrong with all those laid-off U.S. IBM engineers that they couldn't fill the local technical labor demand? They couldn't be *all* bad — after all, they were hired by IBM in the first place and retained for years.

What were unstated in this immigration aspect of the story was not that technical workers were unavailable, but that *cheap* technical workers were unavailable. Lopping off half the technical staff, as Global Services was doing, eliminated much of the company's traditional wisdom and corporate memory in an act that some people, and at least one court, labeled as age discrimination.

The worst part of all was that nobody I talked to who was working at IBM back then thought it would help the business. They believed it would just speed up the death spiral. *Specify the value desired by the customer* was never a consideration. *Manage toward perfection so that the number of steps and the amount of time and information needed to serve the customer continually falls* never happened. In fact it got worse, much worse. It was clear inside IBM that the service to the customer would become significantly worse, and that this would hurt business.

When I wrote about the pending IBM layoffs in May of 2007 and put them in the context of a corporation apparently losing its mind, I evidently struck a chord. Setting some kind of record for reader reaction, I received 1,117 comments. And from the high emotional content of many of those comments, I could see that whatever IBM thought it was doing was causing a great deal of pain and anxiety among IBM employees. IBM as an organization, not just as a business, was seriously in trouble.

Internally IBM denied everything. Here's the message they sent, for example, to every US IBM employee:

05/10/2007 03:57 PM

From: ITD COMM/Somers/IBM

Subject: Rumors of massive layoffs

Patrick Kerin, General Manager, Global Technology Services - Americas

Joanne Collins, Smee General Manager, Integrated Technology Delivery - Americas

Patt Cronin, General Manager, Productivity Initiatives Integrated Technology Delivery

We have received many inquiries regarding the subject. If IBM responded to every rumor, we would get distracted from the important work of delivering value to our clients.

However, a recent external blog report suggesting that IBM is planning a massive layoff is causing unneeded activity. If this blog is generating concern in your unit, please feel free to use this information to assure your teams and business leaders that the blog is inaccurate, and relies on gross exaggerations.

The blog suggested we would be letting go more IBMers than we currently employ in the U.S. The facts are that our regular U.S. population is just under 130,000 IBMers—a number that has remained relatively stable in recent years, as we have divested and acquired businesses and continued to invest through new hiring.

We said when we released 1Q results we would be putting in place a series of actions to address cost issues in our U.S. strategic outsourcing business. We have undertaken efforts toward that, and recently implemented a focused resource reduction in the U.S. While any such reduction is difficult for those employees affected, these actions are well within the scope of our ongoing workforce rebalancing efforts.

The blog also completely misinterpreted our efforts around Lean. To fully understand Lean, you have to view it in a strategic context—a key part of what we're doing to reinvent service delivery to provide more value to clients and make IBM more competitive. We are using Lean, which is a commonly used methodology to conduct process design and development, and to make informed decisions about how to improve and streamline processes. We are going about that in a disciplined and rigorous way, and the intent, as it has always been, is to improve our speed, quality and responsiveness to clients.

And yet IBM never said a word directly to me.

After I sent the company into a tizzy of denial, and then got more reader response, I realized that I wasn't far off with my layoff estimate.

"You were right," said a source back then who still works at IBM. "You called them on the big changes they were planning to make, forcing the company to issue denials, and then drag those changes out over a couple years when they'd intended to impose them all at once. They never thought one blogger could have that much impact."

"You busted us," another IBM sales guy told me, ruefully.

Explain that to my kids, who think I type for a living.

Here's what was happening as I see it now looking back. IBM's mysterious LEAN program was global. LEAN involved the restructuring of IBM's global workforce to achieve certain unstated goals, most likely centered on profitability, with the goal of regaining that 37 percent decrease in market cap IBM had suffered since 1999. The restructuring meant firing employees in some places and hiring them in others.

IBM was and is a true multinational company, and any program like LEAN would have been applied globally. It had to have been since the very essence of IBM's LEAN was foreign hiring. At risk was every non-sales position in IBM Global Services, not just in the U.S., but any country with a cost structure more expensive than the United States, which would include most of Europe and even parts of Asia. At the same time, IBM saw attrition in the U.S. and growth in China and India, so there would probably be significant job losses in the European Union and Japan.

There were two phenomena at work: The low cost of technical labor in certain countries and the general weakness of the U.S. dollar in 2007. IBM profits were up we were told, but if you took into account currency fluctuations, most of IBM's improved financial position (and some could argue most of its profit, period) could be traced to a weak dollar. It wasn't that IBM was so well run, but that the profits it earned in Europe and Japan looked that much larger when brought back to the U.S. and converted into dollars.

Relying on currency fluctuations was not something any company could consistently do to appease Wall Street, which is why IBM's LEAN came about in the first place. But while the weak dollar helped IBM in Europe and Japan, it hurt IBM in the U.S., where Global Services' financial performance had gone from bad to worse.

IBM's U.S. outsourcing business had been declining in the several years before 2007. Through a succession of cost reductions, they were able to partially compensate for the lost profit. But this cost cutting had a negative effect in that it accelerated the loss of business. To make up for such losses, IBM In the early 2000s started its *On Demand* service offering — a computing service based on a utility model. But *On Demand* was not as successful as hoped. It certainly had not replaced the lost services business. So IBM needed a Plan B, and that Plan B was LEAN.

IBM management was impatient and wanted to improve its financial results quickly. They studied the company's situation and probably came up with numeric goals for downsizing and restructuring the company. They used LEAN as a means to get to those goals faster.

Offshoring of some jobs was one way IBM sought to cut costs and improve profitability. Alas, offshoring doesn't work well in practice and certainly doesn't work better than keeping the work here in the US— a fact that IBM and a lot of other companies have consistently failed to see.

IBM claimed in its press release from May 2007—written in frantic and direct response to my blogs on coming IBM layoffs—that they had just under 130,000 IBMers in the United States. Where did I get my estimate of tens of thousands of layoffs? The estimate came from my IBM insiders, who said that the layoff number would include U.S. contractors. If you add them in, the number of IBMers increased considerably. So IBM's number of U.S. workers in their release was misleading at best. But my column was wrong, they said. Life was still good in the world of IBM.

Really?

Then why, instead of coming clean, did the company go underground in late 2007? They simply stopped issuing press releases concerning U.S. layoffs or forced reductions. It's not that the company didn't continue to lose U.S. workers, but just that they stopped talking about it. The company also stopped giving employment numbers by country or, indeed, at all.

And it might have worked, because frankly I didn't want to write about this topic again. I found it depressing. But I had heard from a number of readers asking for an update at the end of 2007. These readers seemed equally divided between men (they were all men) who wanted me to admit I was wrong all along, and other men who seemed to be expecting even more layoffs, and for yet another shoe to fall. Ironically, many of these readers claimed to be IBM employees, even though they were on different sides of the argument. You'd think that as insiders they'd have had a common experience, but they hadn't.

So I took another look at IBM, and what I saw was not pretty. Things were not better. If anything they were worse. Those layoffs I predicted were coming, folks.

IBM had been adding jobs like crazy that year in Argentina, Brazil, China, and India—all low-cost, low-benefit operations. In India alone the company said it had hired 20,000 additional employees in 2007, bringing IBM's Indian employment to 73,000 workers. By the end of 2013, IBM employed more than 100,000 workers in India, which was more than its total direct employment in the United States.

At the time I wrote about this, IBM seemed incapable, however, of producing a number for either its late 2007 U.S. employees, or its total world employment. How was it that the company could know how many workers it employed in India yet not know how many it employed in the United States? A total number of 426,900 IBM workers worldwide finally showed up months later in its annual report for 2007.

Part of the reason so much rancor built up in 2007 with IBM employees is because such hard feelings actually saved the company money. It is always cheaper to get people to quit than to lay them off. Layoffs involve severance payments, retraining, and placement assistance; while quitting requires only accepting an ID badge and locking the door behind the departing employee. More employees quit IBM in 2007 than were laid off, my sources said, and it wasn't hard to see why. The work conditions were poor, and the benefit situation was deteriorating to the extent that for many workers it was probably not worth sticking around. IBM's defined benefit pension plan died in June 2007, for example, and was replaced by a 401K plan.

IBM retirement health care benefits also went in the tank. The company changed the plan for 2007, but made no significant public announcement. Retirees that year were surprised to learn that for some it was now cheaper to buy private health insurance than to go with the IBM plan for retirees. Their benefit was no longer beneficial. This was not retroactive to those previously retired, by the way, or we would have heard an outcry from the tens of thousands of happily retired IBMers from the good old days.

IBM was getting rid of tens of thousands of U.S. jobs yet escaping public attention. Since most of those employees were experienced IT workers, one would assume they could get good jobs. Thanks to the Great Recession and the H-1B visa program, they couldn't. Or if they could, it was with terrible pay. The U.S.A. had more than enough IT workers for its needs. H-1B shut them out of those jobs.

In an election year and with the economy crumbling this could have been a powerful issue, if only politicians had taken the time to understand it. This went *way* beyond IBM. H-1B visa abuse is rampant in high tech where it is used mainly to keep down labor costs – the exact opposite of the stated intent of both the enabling legislation and current political propaganda around proposed immigration reform. There is no high-tech labor shortage in America no matter what industry says.

But IBM was, and is, the poster child for bad management. IBM's leadership appeared transfixed on two things—selling and cutting costs.

They were pushing their sales force very hard, and squeezing commissions at the same time. They were cutting everyone and everything.

What IBM did not understand was how to run a business. All parts of the company should have been generating revenue. Leadership should have been coaching and facilitating this effort. Every line of business should have been constantly monitored, and adjustments made to ensure short-term and long-term success. IBM really didn't do this. All decisions came from the top. There was no delegation of authority. Business units had floundered for years from neglect. When their financials began to fail, they got lots of help, and the wrong kind of help, from the top.

Sadly, many IBMers in Europe, Asia, and South America thought they were the future of the company. They saw the big USA job cuts as proof *they* were better. But they weren't better, just cheaper. IBM management wasn't going to listen to them either. In the end it was the *customer* who paid IBM's bills and everyone's paychecks. It was not IBM or Wall Street.

Business is about keeping customers happy, a trick the guys in Armonk seemed to have forgotten. When would they remember? Well, at the dawn of 2008, they hadn't yet.

A thought about the survivors:

Survivors are those technical people at IBM who didn't get the axe. If the company's motivation was purely financial, wasn't everyone equally exposed to layoffs? Hardly. Most of the people I spoke to at IBM in May of 2007 hadn't lost their jobs, nor were they even in danger of losing their jobs. I tried to speak to the people best qualified to comment, and, in this case, they were the ones generally charged with making the new system work. IBM isn't stupid. The company made an effort to pursue LEAN in a way that caused as little collateral damage as possible, which meant relying even more on its strongest contributors. And these very able, if harried, folks had a fair chance of saving the day. But they weren't whining to me; they were annoyed. They were tired of *having to save the day*. These were people all of us could admire and most of us would be better for emulating. And that made their reluctantly held positions all the more eloquent.

Here's how one IBM employee put it as he resigned: "Unfortunately, I see IBM as a place run by salespeople and project managers with a sell-and-install mentality, even in services. There is no technical leadership, innovation or proper understanding of our customer's needs and requirements. The architecture profession is dysfunctional and cannot remediate itself. These factors may change, but not in the short term and when it does, it is likely to be brutal, and I'm not patient enough to wait around."

And this from another IBMer who, at the time, was sticking around: "As part of the cost cutting, IBM cut some of its billable rates to help get business. The problem is, consultants are expected to bill more and more hours to make up for the lower rates. For some (including myself), we're expected to bill 93.5 percent of 2,080 hours yearly. The problem is, when you factor in vacation, a sick day or two, etc., that leaves almost no spare time. What's happening is that IBM is no longer providing training to their consultants, expecting us to pick things up on our own. This is leading to a much lower quality of work on projects.

"In addition, the demand for more billable hours is resulting in some ethically questionable actions. Starting four weeks before the end of each quarter, we start getting emails asking us to try and bill more hours. They always include statements saying 'to help improve customer satisfaction and meet deadlines,' but with a wink-wink, it's implied that you add on an extra hour or two. The resulting billable hour crunch has also led to less people exceeding or meeting their goals, leading to an overall lower yearly bonus (called variable pay).

"Many people are quitting IBM, and IBM is now in a hiring crunch because it can't fill projects. The result is that they're stuffing anyone available onto projects (regardless of skill level), again lowering the quality of our deliverables. The lowering of bonuses and increased utilization has prompted many former PriceWaterhouseCoopers people to jump ship. So, IBM is sacrificing the long-term health of IBM Global Services, to keep up the quarter-to-quarter results."

IBM — 15 years undoing a century of accomplishments

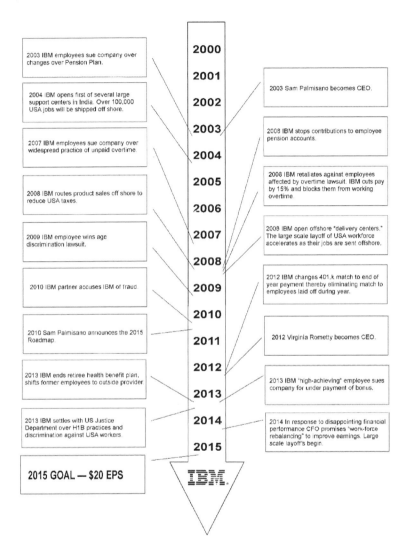

2003 IBM employees sue company over changes over Pension Plan.

2004 IBM opens first of several large support centers in India. Over 100,000 USA jobs will be shipped off shore.

2007 IBM employees sue company over widespread practice of unpaid overtime.

2008 IBM routes product sales off shore to reduce USA taxes.

2009 IBM employee wins age discrimination lawsuit.

2010 IBM partner accuses IBM of fraud.

2010 Sam Palmisano announces the 2015 Roadmap.

2013 IBM ends retiree health benefit plan, shifts former employees to outside provider.

2013 IBM settles with US Justice Department over H1B practices and discrimination against USA workers.

2015 GOAL — $20 EPS

2000
2001
2002
2003
2004
2005
2006
2007
2008
2009
2010
2011
2012
2013
2014
2015

IBM.

2003 Sam Palmisano becomes CEO.

2008 IBM stops contributions to employee pension accounts.

2008 IBM retaliates against employees affected by overtime lawsuit. IBM cuts pay by 15% and blocks them from working overtime.

2008 IBM open offshore "delivery centers." The large scale layoff of USA workforce accelerates as their jobs are sent offshore.

2012 IBM changes 401.k match to end of year payment thereby eliminating match to employees laid off during year.

2012 Virginia Rometty becomes CEO.

2013 IBM "high-achieving" employee sues company for under payment of bonus.

2014 In response to disappointing financial performance CFO promises "work-force rebalancing" to improve earnings. Large scale layoff's begin.

6

'DEATH MARCH 2015'

In April 2012, I reminded readers about IBM's internal plan to grow earnings-per-share to $20 by 2015. The primary method for accomplishing this feat, according to the plan, would be by reducing the U.S. employee head count by up to 78 percent in that time frame. (In 2013, IBM said its worldwide employee headcount was 434,000, and, in 2012, 435,000. IBM still does not break out numbers of U.S. employees.)

The plan was still on track and it still left me puzzled. Who, under this plan, would still be a U.S. IBM employee in 2015? Top management would remain, the sales organization would endure, as would employees working on U.S. government contracts that require workers to be U.S citizens. Everyone else would be gone—everyone.

Industries and businesses change all the time because they have to or want to. Big companies and small have to adjust to the realities and changing reward structures of their markets and cultures. Or they change to better adapt to new opportunities. But what was happening at IBM was different than that. And it was different because this incredible American success story of a company, if it continued to follow its current course, would utterly fail. It was different, too, because neither IBM executive management nor Wall Street seemed to have the slightest notion of the peril facing the company.

IBM appeared to believe it was cheaper to replace a skilled worker with two or three unskilled or less skilled workers to do the same job. That is like hiring nine women to make a baby in one month. While it looks interesting on paper, it does not work. The language barrier for IBM's Indian staff is huge, for example. Troubleshooting, which was once performed on conference calls, is now done with instant messaging because the teams speak so poorly. Problems that an experienced person could fix in a few minutes are taking an army of folks *hours* to fix. This is infuriating and alarming to IBM's customers, longtime IBMers tell me.

"This low-cost, no-experience global resourcing strategy is not limited to the services part of IBM," one veteran of 30 years wrote. "It is hitting product development, maintenance and support, with the result of products that are so bad they cannot be sold, or have to be rewritten by experienced people in the United States, the United Kingdom, Canada, Japan, Germany, and other highly developed nations.

"It is also hitting virtually all IBM processes that effect customers from sales, to ordering, to fulfillment, to billing, to service," the reader continued. "Literally everything that effects IBM internally and IBM clients/customers is being off-shored as fast as possible to cut costs.

"I see the effects and the failures of this daily. Customers are leaving, and others are upset and suing, or threatening to do so. These resources cannot do the job, yet IBM rewards them by giving these incompetents more work to do. The executives literally do not give a damn. All that matters are the short-term numbers, making that 2015 target, and collecting their bonuses.

"We have our own name for the 2015 Roadmap—we call it *Death March 2015*."

IBM's five-year plan ending in 2010 doubled earnings per share from just less than $5 to about $11. In 2013, it was about $15. (In May 2014, it is closer to $14.) During that five-year period, there was an accelerated push of jobs offshore for cost reasons; there were high attrition rates, and longer product release cycles. So will the five-year-plan will really double EPS to about $20? Maybe, but, as I've said, the particular way they are going about it is also likely to destroy IBM.

Some analysts, and thus, the business press, are finally seeing the light about IBM's self-induced injuries. At IBM's May 14, 2014 meeting with financial analysts, several analysts expressed doubts that IBM could make its $20 EPS projection, partly because of eight straight quarters of declining sales. One analyst estimated that IBM would report adjusted earnings of $17.80 at year's end, missing its target of $18.

"We remain concerned that while IBM is re-inventing parts of its product portfolio, it is not moving fast enough to keep up with industry changes and grow both revenue and gross margins," ISI Group analyst Brian Marshall wrote in a note to his clients. Ben Reitzes, an analyst at Barclays Plc., suggested Rometty should drop her 2015 earnings target and focus on the transition to cloud computing and other new product sales. CEO Rometty, in a rare public appearance, reiterated her stance that the 2015 $20 per share goal was still on target.

But back to why I think IBM will destroy itself. IBM's biggest moneymaker is Global Services, which also employs the most people. But the company is now making a lot less on its contracts, and the turnover of business is brisk. It is in Global Services where you see the most jobs being shipped offshore. But the problem is the offshore teams often lack the skill and experience to do the work — problems mount, and customers like The Walt Disney Company get upset and leave.

This is unfair to customers and simply stupid. When I wrote about IBM in 2007, LEAN was supposed to mold from Big Blue a hyper-efficient business machine through vast layoffs. Yet today IBM has many more layers of management than it had in 2007. These extra layers come at a cost both in dollars and accountability, and they insulate IBM's top management from responsibility for their decisions. At the highest levels in Armonk, they think things are going beautifully because executives are out of touch with the reality of their own company.

Today at IBM, the U.S. workers who speak out and try to save the business are the first in line to lose their jobs. Management accountability is gone. The people who mess up get to keep their jobs; and those trying to retain the business lose their jobs.

Something's Rotten in Dubuque.

IBM's 2015 plan to deliver earnings-per-share was announced to the delight of Wall Street, and IBMers were offered a carrot, a few shares of stock to be granted at the end of 2015 as a reward for helping achieve that target. It appears that IBM's goal was not to issue many of those grants as they continued to conduct **resource actions** (IBM-speak for permanent layoffs) and remove talented and valuable U.S. employees in favor of moving work to low-cost countries such as Brazil, Argentina, India, and China.

Work that stays onshore is mainly sent to what are called Global Delivery Facilities (GDFs), two of which were created at heritage IBM locations (Poughkeepsie, N.Y. and Boulder, Colo.) while new ones were starting in Dubuque, Iowa and in Columbia, Mo. IBM's public position in 2010 was they were creating jobs in smaller towns, when in fact they were displacing workers from other parts of the United States by moving jobs to these GDFs or to offshore locations.

In the case of Dubuque and Columbia, IBM secured heavy incentives from state and local governments to minimize their costs in these locations, and were achieving further savings by paying the technical team members — most of whom were new hires or fresh college grads with no experience — a fraction of what experienced support personnel would require.

Let's look closer at Dubuque, not because it is any different from the rest of IBM USA but simply, to characterize the company at a finer scale. When IBM opened the Dubuque center, the people of Iowa were expecting great things. The center was staffed by a small number of U.S. IBMers in management positions. IBM then brought over people from India for training, and then sent them home. Few H-1B visas were even required.

Every time IBM sent a batch of trainees back to India from Iowa they laid off more U.S. workers. While the city of Dubuque was led to believe they'd get an influx of highly paid new residents, what the city actually received was a transient workforce of underpaid expats — workers that may well be invisible to local government. It would be interesting to know now how many permanent hires in Dubuque were Iowa residents or graduates of Iowa universities. How many workers spent less than a year in Dubuque? Did Iowa see any benefit from the investment they made to open the IBM Dubuque center?

Whenever IBM has a big new project they now have to bring in extra workers, usually from India. I have been told the company plans the arrivals carefully so that they occur over several days, or even stretch to a few weeks. They route arriving workers through different airports. They make sure there are never more than two or three workers coming on the same flight, effectively avoiding notice by Immigration and Homeland Security. Are any of these workers paying FICA or U.S. income taxes? Good question. Why is IBM sneaking around? Better question.

With hundreds of thousands of laid-off IT workers in the United States, why can't IBM hire American workers for these positions? That appears to be because IBM doesn't want U.S. employees, who cost more than overseas workers. They don't want European employees either for the same reason, and because Europeans are also harder to jettison.

Today, IBM does have many American employees working in its GDCs. Some of these workers are contractors. All of them are paid significantly below market rates. Recently, to reduce costs, IBM has been laying off or furloughing its contractors and forcing direct employees to work very long hours with no overtime, no pay increases, and no bonuses. Since the economic crisis of 2008, jobs are very hard to find, and IBM is using this situation to take every advantage of its workforce it can.

Layoffs at IBM are rarely due to job performance, though complaining will get you sacked. IBM tends to position these actions as job eliminations, but jobs aren't usually eliminated, they are just sent to locations staffed by cheaper workers. IBM manages to skirt the Worker Adjustment and Retraining Notification (WARN) Act, which requires advance notification of layoffs or plant closings, by instead structuring these resource actions to stay just below the numbers required to provide notifications at given locations. In this way IBM has managed to avoid criticism from the mainstream media, and touts itself as a good corporate citizen while continuing to expect remaining employees to work 60 to 70 or more hours per week to keep up with the amount of work.

These draconian tactics might be justified if survival of the company or the best interests of the customer were involved, but they aren't. It's mainly about executive compensation. Meanwhile, IBM's work for customers is becoming increasingly shoddy. Contract terms such as vulnerability scanning, ID re-validations, and security implementations are routinely late or not done properly. Account teams are under continued pressure to meet revenue and cost targets regardless of how poorly the contracts were structured by the original sales team. Each business sector has a target to move a certain percentage of their technical work to an offshore Global Resource Center or to an onshore GDF.

IBM's goal appears to be to have as few employees in the U.S. as possible, maximizing profit. But doing so clearly hurts customer satisfaction.

Major IBM customers such as Amgen Inc., The State of Texas, and Walt Disney Co. cut ties with IBM in favor of other providers in 2012. Other customers are scaling back the services they're buying from IBM as perceived value continues to drop. Customers are starting to realize that they can hire offshore IT service companies such as TCS, Wipro, HCL and Satyam and book the savings directly instead of paying IBM top dollar for support and then seeing that support fulfilled from Brazil, India and China. Why pay IBM $60 to $100 an hour for $8-to-$15 help when you can hire higher quality $20-an- hour help directly?

When IBM first started its big push to offshore technical work, the account teams were asked to make a list of reasons why customers' work couldn't be off-shored, but were not allowed to use skills as a reason. That makes no sense in a rational organization, but it makes perfect sense to IBM.

The current irrationality at IBM is not new. Big Blue has been in crazy raptures before. One was the development of the System 360 in the 1960s when T.J. Watson Jr. bet the company and won big; though it took two tries and almost killed the outfit along the way. So there's a legacy of heroic miracles at IBM, though it has been a long while since one really paid off.

There are those who would strongly disagree with this last statement. They'd say that IBM, with its strong financial performance, is right now in one of its greater moments. But haven't we just seen that's not true? Successful companies aren't heartsick and self-destructive, and IBM today is exactly that, so the company is not a success.

Considering the way the company is being run, where will future IBM growth come from? Wherever it comes from, can IBM execute on its plan to grow new businesses using cheap, under-skilled offshore talent? If Global Services is struggling to hang on, how well will this work for the new IBM growth businesses coming up? As IBM infuriates more and more of its customers, how long can IBM expect to keep selling big-ticket products and services to those very same customers?

Global Services is a mature business that has been around for 23 years. In IBM's 2015 business plan, big income is expected from newer IBM businesses like Business Analytics, Cloud, Smarter Computing, and Smarter Planet. Can these businesses be grown in three to five years into the multi-billion-dollar level of gross profit coming from Global Services? Most of these businesses are tiny. A few of them are not even well conceived as businesses. It takes special skills and commitment to grow a business from nothing to the $1 billion range. IBM probably doesn't have what it takes.

Do you remember *eBusiness*? (A termed coined by IBM in 1997 that meant transforming key business processes using Internet technologies.) And I've already mentioned On Demand, the utility computing service system for large enterprises. These are examples of businesses IBM planned to grow to billions in sales, but are businesses that no longer even exist today. The Blue Gene supercomputer project belongs here, too.

Here's a simple thought experiment:

When it comes to these new software and Internet services, IBM's competition comes from a variety of companies including Amazon, Apple, Dell, Google, Hewlett Packard, Oracle and others. Does IBM have an inherent advantage at this point against any of those companies? No. Is IBM in any way superior to all of them and thence in a position to claim dominance? No.

IBM isn't smarter, richer, faster moving, or better connected. They may be willing to promise more, but if they can't also deliver on those promises, any advantage disappears.

Of course IBM is still buying profitable businesses, and imposing on them IBM processes, cutting costs and squeezing profits until customers inevitably disappear and it is time to buy another company. It's a survival technique but hardly a recipe for greatness.

My opinion is that IBM's services business profit will continue to decline as they try to cost-cut into prosperity. Unless they find a way to grow revenue and provide a quality product or service, they're headed for a sell-off of the entire service business. With earnings-per-share meaning everything to the nobility, and a headcount mandate that can't be achieved without totally transforming the company, IBM is turning itself into something very different. Gerstner's service business that saved the company 20 years ago will be eventually jettisoned, probably to a combination of U.S. and international buyers.

The Global Services business could be sold to one or more Indian companies while the current federal business could be sold to one of IBM's U.S. competitors. Meanwhile, IBM will move its business toward hardware and applications delivered by vendor partners who will carry the Service Level Agreement (SLA) penalty risk. In short, it's a race to the bottom and only IBM executives are winning. Ultimately it will be IBM's customers, employees, and shareholders who will be the losers.

Yes, but some readers tell me, that's just services, not the real IBM.

There is no real IBM — not any longer.

The company has become a cash cow. In IBM's view, you never feed a cash cow — just take money out until the cow is dead.

Before we move on, let's examine that SLA penalty issue because I think there's an aspect of this that's misunderstood in the marketplace. More than a decade ago, in one of those "Aha!" moments that transform corporations, IBM figured out that it was better to ask forgiveness from its customers than to ask permission. Specifically, IBM considered two competing scenarios:

1) Follow service agreements to the letter.

2) Ignore service agreements (guaranteeing specific uptime percentages, for example, or repairs within a certain time frame), thus saving money, and expect to pay penalties as a result.

IBM decided it could make more money — a lot more money — by paying penalties than by actually doing what it was being paid to do.

Just like Ford deciding it was cheaper for a few customers to die than to improve Pinto fuel tank safety, IBM decided to deliberately cheat its customers. It came down to an actuarial decision, that maybe customers wouldn't notice or even ask for IBM to pay penalties, and that any penalties, if ever applied, would cost IBM less than the contracted work the company wasn't really bothering to do.

Here's a look at this customer service problem from the inside, circa April 2014, courtesy of a current worker at one of IBM's Global Delivery Centers:

"Aside from laying off a bunch of people, they are furloughing all the contractors, and stating we cannot have overtime. Half of my team is out, and this whole no overtime thing, with no night staff, page-out requirements, and off-hour change windows all mean there is usually no one in on Fridays to work. In fact, I think having someone arrange a tour within the Global Technology Services part of IBM at any facility on a Friday would be an eye opener — lots of empty desks. Clients pay per full-time equivalent (FTE) jobs and IBM is supposed to staff that, but I know of a team that supports 40 clients with 16 people. Just one of that team's clients is supposed to have 10 FTE. A customer might be told that they have seven people with IDs that can work on a project, but aren't told those seven people have eight other clients. They're scamming the customers, basically."

Not only is IBM scamming its Global Services customers, but the company is scamming itself. IBM outsourcing teams used to generate a lot of new business. In addition to supporting customer systems, they helped with sales and consulting. With sales a customer could buy new, often complex technology and IBM would set it up for them well. When the consultants sold new ideas, having a strong team that could execute their projects was invaluable. Now the reverse is happening. The outsourcing organization is crippled, which is hurting system and software sales. Projects are failing.

One reason IBM's revenue is dropping is because the outsourcing business is deeply damaged. If IBM cannot execute projects and support what it sells, those big future lines of business are at risk of failure.

7

A TALE OF TWO
DIVISION SALES

To see how far IBM has already fallen and how far from reality corporate thinking in Armonk is, let's compare the sale of two IBM divisions: the 2004 sale of the IBM PC division to China's Lenovo, and the 2014 pending sale of IBM's Intel server business, also to Lenovo. The two sales efforts couldn't be more different, and the trend is very disturbing.

When IBM announced what was then its Entry Systems Division and introduced to the world the underpowered, overpriced, but fantastically successful IBM Personal Computer, China wasn't even a major trading partner with the US. The simple story of selling the division twenty-four years later — and the only story that made it in most papers — was that IBM hadn't made much of a profit on PC products for years, so selling out was a simple way of improving corporate results and shifting capital to where it could be used more profitably.

Well, yes and no. PCs had become a commodity, true, and IBM hadn't made money on them since the late 1980s, but the story went far beyond raising gross margins and cutting pension liabilities.

Take a look at the sale price, for one thing. The mix of cash and stock and assumption of debt amounted to about $1.8 billion, which was a lot of money. But remember, this was for a chunk of IBM that produced

$9.2 billion in sales in 2003. Setting the price at 20 percent of sales sure seemed low, even if there was little profit. The question that ought to have been asked at the time, but wasn't, was: "What would Carly Fiorina (then-CEO of Hewlett-Packard) have paid for the same property?" Fiorina, who paid $25 billion for Compaq Computer in 2001, would certainly have paid two to three times what Lenovo had for the chance to leapfrog Dell and become the world's largest producer of personal computers, along with the largest computer company of any kind, at least at the time.

Okay, so IBM didn't want to make HP an even bigger competitor, then why didn't it sell to a big Japanese player like NEC, which had paid more than $1.8 billion for little Packard Bell? The dollar was down, the yen was up, and the cost of corporate borrowing in Japan was almost free—so why didn't IBM sell to a Japanese company? Or to a European one? Or even to another American company? Gateway Inc. paid more cash for eMachines than Lenovo paid for IBM. Wouldn't former Gateway CEO and Chairman Ted Waitt have ponied-up big bucks for the use of the IBM brand? Of course he would have. (Gateway was the PC company known for its down-home branding, complete with computer boxes patterned with black and white Holstein Cow patterns. Acer Inc. bought Gateway in 2007, although Gateway retained the name and still does business as Gateway Inc.).

What was absolutely key to the IBM PC deal was that the buyer was Lenovo, then the largest Chinese PC maker, and now the largest PC maker in the world. Yes, IBM's PC division was unprofitable and IBM would have eventually had to do something about it, but Sam Palmisano wanted a Chinese buyer and was willing to accept far less cash than he might have received elsewhere just to get the buyer he wanted. IBM got rid of a headache, and in doing so, gained unique access to what would eventually become be the world's largest IT market. This deal was all about China, not the US.

It's best to do business in China with a partner. You don't just set up an IBM China and start selling stuff. You find a partner company and move into the market together. IBM's partner was Lenovo, which was a good partner to have. IBM not only had its Chinese partner, it had a substantial equity position in that partner as a result of this transaction. That was unique as far as I knew at the time. Chinese-US corporate partnerships aren't always the easiest marriages, but in this one IBM actually had a vote. At the time, it also got Lenovo to move its global headquarters to the US and accept an American CEO and 10,000 U.S. employees.

In any other U.S.-China corporate partnership, a top-level meeting requires a 20-hour plane ride, but the top guys at IBM and Lenovo could meet for lunch at Denny's. All this was nothing but good for IBM.

Under the agreement, IBM retained design input on future PC products, which continued to carry the IBM brand for five years. In that short time the company had severed any major financial dependence on the future of those product lines. In short, this was the end of the line for IBM's marriage with Intel. Sure, they continued to sell boxes containing Intel (and perhaps AMD) processors, but the historic link was severed, with the result that IBM was able to compete with impunity using its own PowerPC and Power5 processors.

Palmisano essentially cleared the decks so he could compete unfettered in a completely different segment of the market—servers— where IBM once made money, and where they proceeded at the time to crush the competition. Winners in this deal were IBM, Lenovo, AMD, and Dell. Lenovo instantly doubled its market share. AMD ate away just a little bit more at Intel's power base. Dell, as the true PC market leader back then, relied on its lower overhead to try and further hurt HP. Losers in the deal were HP, Intel, and Sun—especially Sun. Those guys were in trouble.

Palmisano was savvy enough to sell to Lenovo in 2004, but when Ginni Rometty tried to make a similar move earlier this year, negotiating the proposed sale of IBM's Intel server business to Lenovo, she made a big mistake.

If the sale is completed, IBM selling its Intel server business to Lenovo is yet another example of Big Blue eating its seed corn, effectively dooming the company for the sake of short-term earnings. It would be a good move for Lenovo but an act of desperation for IBM. Many Wall Street analysts saw the proposed sale as good, but sometimes Wall Street analysts aren't that smart. They characterized it as selling off a low-margin server business (Intel-based servers) to concentrate on a higher-margin server business (z-series and p-series big iron) but the truth was IBM is proposing to sell its future to invest in its past. Little servers are the future of big computing. IBM needs to be a major supplier and a major player in this emerging market if it is going to be a factor at all.

If you look at the technology used today by Google, Yahoo, and Amazon and many others like Intel, and Sun, you'll see it is possible to operate a large enterprise on huge arrays of inexpensive Intel servers.

For a fraction of the cost of an IBM z-Series (mainframe) or p-Series (mid-range Unix) system, equivalent computer power can be assembled from a modest number of low-cost servers and new software tools. IBM will have turned its back on this truth if the Intel server business sale goes through.

Maybe this wouldn't matter if IBM was selling a lot of those higher-margin Z- and P-series machines, but from the look of their latest earnings statements I don't think that's the case. So they are essentially selling a lower-margin business, where customers are actually buying, to invest in a higher-margin business where customers aren't buying.

Yeah, right.

Information Technology is entering a commodity era of computing. Mainframes, mid-range computers and servers are becoming commodities and IBM needs to learn how to operate in a commodity market. IBM needs to become the lowest cost, highest volume producer of commodity servers. PureSystems is an IBM product line of factory pre-configured components and servers also being referred to as an "Expert Integrated System", according to Wikipedia. But developing new million-dollar PureSystems will not bring the business needed to IBM's Systems and Technology group.

Somebody in Armonk has to know this, right?

IBM needs to embrace the new era of large arrays of inexpensive Intel servers. IBM needs to adapt its mainframe and mid-range applications to this new platform. The world is moving in this direction. Selling the Intel server business would be exactly the wrong thing to do for the long-term health of IBM.

Inexpensive servers do not necessarily have to be Intel-based either. IBM could become the leader of large arrays of inexpensive Power- and ARM-based servers. The market is moving to commodity processors. IBM needs to evolve too, and be part of that future. But as the Intel server sales show, they aren't evolving and won't evolve. And this is another reason I fear the company is doomed.

8

FINANCIAL
ENGINEERING

If, as is the case at IBM, the primary corporate goal is to hit a certain earnings target set years before by a guy who no longer even works at the company, you'd better have some powerful financial tools to help the company get there. Growing earnings-per-share can be done by increasing profits, by decreasing the number of outstanding shares or by a combination of both techniques. IBM, faced as it has been in recent years with flat to declining sales, has attempted to do both while throwing in at the same time a huge dose of corporate cost cutting. If you ever wonder how the Tea Party would run America, just look at IBM.

Much of the rest of this book deals with how the company is attempting to grow sales and cut costs, but this little chapter is devoted solely to the other side of the equation—the reduction of outstanding shares. If you spread declining profits across a pile of shares that is getting smaller even faster, that, my friends, is called earnings growth. Yeah, right.

The number of outstanding shares is reduced through buying them back from existing shareholders. This is often presented as a really good idea because it effectively gives money back to shareholders through what's presented as a more tax-efficient manner than a simple stock dividend. With a dividend, you see, IBM would first pay corporate income tax on the money, possibly reducing the total sum available to be distributed to shareholders. And when the dividends were distributed to shareholders they'd pay income taxes on it again—double taxation. Shareholder buybacks, then, ought to allow shareholders to receive more money and pay less tax on that money because it is taxed only once at the lower capital gains rate, and shareholders who don't want to sell shares back aren't required to. This is the sort of gambit reformed corporate raider Carl Icahn loved to push on the companies in which he invested.

IBM, unlike some of the Icahn target companies like Apple and eBay, isn't at all resistant to buying back its own shares. In the last decade, in fact, IBM has spent $101 billion buying back shares, thereby reducing the number outstanding by about a third. But there's something odd about the way IBM buys back its own shares: The company does it with borrowed money.

The usual scenario in share buybacks is that the company has too much cash on its books and that cash could be better used by shareholders than by the company. IBM is carrying plenty of cash, too, but still the company borrows what it needs for share buybacks. I can't see borrowing money to buy back shares unless those shares are at a discount price, which IBM's in the last five years have mainly not been. Why do they borrow the money?

Trying to understand this whole share buyback business I turned to my old friend Ray Ostby, a longtime Silicon Valley chief financial officer recently retired. Ray, who started his high tech career as assistant CFO at Intel before going on to the big jobs at many other companies in the Valley, tried to guide me. But I have to admit it wasn't easy because when it comes to Generally Accepted Accounting Principles (GAAP) what makes sense doesn't always make sense.

For example, that borrowed $101 billion ($8 billion in the first quarter of 2014 alone), is a heck of a lot of money. What if IBM didn't buy back shares at all, wouldn't that $101 billion or $8 billion flow through as profit, or at least the interest paid (or not paid, in this case) would, right?

Nope.

"Money spent on a stock buy-back is not an expense on the P&L at all, ever, never," said Ray. "Not having repurchased shares would not increase net income. Capital transactions do not flow through the income statement." So what looks like a smoking gun might be smoking, but it isn't a gun.

"They seem to spend their net income each year buying back shares (plus or minus, but within a margin)," Ray continued. "They seem to borrow money at the beginning of the year to fund the buy-back program, and they seem to repay that debt during the year as the income is realized. That is, they don't seem to build insurmountable debt for this program. The only justification for a buy-back program is that the shareholder can make more with the cash than the company can. That means that they must have decided that they can't earn more than the S&P 500 either because their products or markets have matured, so they now have diminishing returns, or their management is complacent and not aggressive enough. So, to achieve EPS growth, they've decided that they can't increase the numerator significantly so they are trying to decrease the denominator.

"This is a reasonable approach for any company that bloats their outstanding shares with stock option plans, stock purchase plans and M&A with stock. And as you've said previously, management bonuses are probably tied to increased share price. **You get what you incentivize.**"

"It makes no sense," agreed Roger Martin, the business professor from Toronto, "except for stock-based compensated executives. For them it makes all the sense in the whole wide world."

There's an odd dichotomy here that IBM presents itself as an aggressive, thoroughly modern technology company, yet implicit in its gleeful embrace of share buybacks is the admission that the company can't see how it can natively return more on the money than could the S&P 500 index. If there's an irony here it's that this shouldn't be true. IBM should be able to do better with the money than its shareholders can.

"I still say that there is a place for buybacks, but not in lieu of operating performance," said Ray Ostby. "It should be in addition to better performance. I am surprised that IBM increased their debt to increase buybacks. They seem now to be addicted to the debt." (The full analogy is that drugs feel good for a while until the user needs more to sustain the same high, and then the user spirals out of control. It looks like they continued borrowing beyond their ability to re-pay in the same business cycle.)

"IBM should consider using its cash to make more acquisitions that will help it grow. It also seems that the Board gave the CEO an EPS target without a revenue or gross margin or operating margin target. These goals shouldn't be issued in a vacuum. The fact that they'd had year after year of sales declines for eight straight quarters meant that their core businesses were either mature, or not being well executed, or both."

Economist David Stockman looks deeper into the IBM buyback strategy in his book *The Great Deformation*, blaming it on easy money policy from the U.S. Federal Reserve Bank. "During the seven years ending in 2013 IBM booked about $100 billion in net income," Stockman writes, "and **spent virtually every single penny on share buy backs**. So the once and former king of the global high-tech industry had nothing better to do with its cash than shrink its equity base. Accordingly, its share count dropped by 20 percent over the period, thereby accounting for about 45 percent of its EPS growth. Moreover, it also distributed another $20 billion in dividends over the 7-year period. In all, it delivered cash into the maws of the fast money and hedge fund complex that amounted to 120 percent of its net income for 2007-2013. Needless to say, the robo traders can never get enough of this kind of 'shareholder friendly' action at any given moment in time–no matter that it amounts to corporate liquidation eventually."

Stockman further relates IBM's efforts to drop its effective corporate tax rates down to 15.5 percent in 2013 from 28 percent in 2007 to its acquisition strategy over the same period. He claims that had IBM not worked so hard to drive down its tax rate, 2013 EPS would have been $9.50 rather than $15. Stockman goes on to observe that IBM's acquisitions over this period were **"inherently and prodigiously "accretive" to per share earnings not because they make any economic sense, but because its after-tax cost of debt capital is nearly zero."**

Conservative economist Stockman isn't arguing that companies ought to pay higher taxes than they have to or pay more for acquisitions than they need to, nor am I. What I believe we are both pointing out here is that IBM management has put most of its effort over the past several years into increasing earnings through financial shenanigans rather than leveraging its historical strengths and **building the business.** "It becomes quickly evident that EPS accretion on an accounting basis may have virtually no relationship whatsoever to genuine corporate value creation -- the ostensible point of the mindless M&As that preoccupy the C-suites of corporate America.," Stockman writes. "...it might by questioned how a technology giant can prosper over time by consuming 15 percent of its capital assets each and every year." **I don't believe they can, which is why IBM is headed off a cliff.**

Meanwhile, here is the long-awaited IBM stock chart with a little analysis of Big Blue's stock market success through the Great Recession when most other IT companies dropped sharply but IBM shares actually went up. Was this rise another miracle of Palmisano's Nobel-worthy corporate stewardship? Probably not. IBM management thinks Sam's leadership and business plan were great because the stock price soared when most others soured. They didn't know trillions of dollars of investments fled the stock market after the crash. As a broadly hedged multinational, IBM was a safe investment and a lot of investors flocked to it. If system sales were slow that must have been someone's fault. They tend to forget that there was a financial disaster, and that the whole business world is still in shock.

IBM didn't even understand its own success.

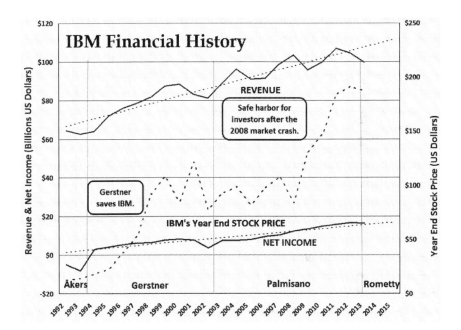

9

AN IT LABOR ECONOMICS LESSON FROM MEMPHIS FOR IBM

My columns on troubles at IBM brought many sad stories from customers burned by Big Blue. Then a truly teachable lesson emerged from a couple of those horror tales, and it had to do with US IT labor economics and immigration policy, especially H-1B guest worker visas.

The story about H-1B visas is simple. H-1Bs are given for foreign workers to fill U.S. positions that can't be filled with qualified US citizens or by permanent US residents who hold green cards. H-1Bs came into existence because there weren't enough green cards, and now we're told there aren't enough H-1Bs, either. So there's a more or less continual move in Washington to increase the H-1B limit above the current level of approximately 65,000 per year because we are told **the alternative is IT paralysis without more foreign workers.**

Says who?

Cynics like me point out that foreign workers are paid less, and more importantly, place much less of a total financial burden on employers because they get few, if any, long term benefits. I tend to think the issue isn't finding good workers, but finding cheaper workers. However the H-1B program by law isn't supposed to be about saving money, so that argument can't be used by organizations pushing for higher visa limits. All they can claim is a labor shortage that can only be corrected by issuing more H-1Bs.

To test this theory let's look at Memphis, Tenn., where IBM in 2012 lost two big customers: Hilton Hotels and ServiceMaster.

Hilton canceled almost all of their contracts with IBM less than two years into a five-year deal. This included global IT help desk, all data centers, and support of "global web" (hilton.com and all related systems). According to my sources at Hilton, the IBM contract was a nightmare. IBM couldn't keep Hilton's Exchange servers running. The Storage Area Network (SAN) in IBM's own Raleigh data center hadn't worked right since it was installed, with some SAN outages lasting more than a day. IBM couldn't monitor Hilton's servers in the IBM data center. Hilton had to tell IBM when the servers were running low on disk space, for example.

IBM had massive outages at Hilton. During one several-day outage in 2011, when you called to get a reservation you were routed to the hotel and the hotel worker checked their clipboard. At the check-in process they would pick your room from another clipboard. A Hilton employee would then physically check your room to make sure no one else was using it. Imagine if this were your hotel or your business—how would you feel?

Inside IBM the problems on the Hilton account were well known and often discussed. Many in IBM knew how poorly IBM was serving this customer. Yet IBM leadership refused to make things right. It was better for IBM to let Hilton crash and burn.

Now IBM is gone, replaced by Dell, and Hilton has a new CIO. I guess the old adage "Nobody ever got fired for buying from IBM" is no longer correct.

If there's one point I'd like you to keep in mind about this Hilton story it is IBM's apparent inability to monitor the Hilton servers, which I will talk about more below.

ServiceMaster, another former IBM customer in Memphis is a privately held provider of services to homes and businesses including such brands as Terminix, American Home Shield, and Merry Maids. Among its many beefs with IBM, ServiceMaster also had a server monitoring issue. In this case it involved the database for one of ServiceMaster's major business applications. Different groups monitored the servers, operating systems, storage, and databases. **Most of the**

monitoring was done manually, and sometimes not at all. The primary way IBM would know there was a problem was when ServiceMaster complained. One evening during an application "change," something went wrong and the database was corrupted. The failover of the database to the back-up system failed. The disaster recovery plan failed. IBM then tried to restore the database from its back-up tapes, but that recovery process failed. Business data was lost, and IBM brought in data experts to try to recover and reconstruct the lost data, but they failed and the data was lost forever.

In this case it was the company's main database — its commercial lifeblood — that was going unmonitored. IBM was supposed to be monitoring the servers, and they were *paid* for monitoring the servers, but, in fact, IBM didn't really monitor anything and instead relied on help desk trouble tickets to tell it when there was a problem. If you think about it, this is exactly the way IBM was handling server problems at Hilton, too.

Now to the part about labor economics.

When ServiceMaster announced its decision to cancel its contract with IBM and to bring in a new IT team, the company had to immediately find 200 solid IT people. Memphis is a small community and there can't be that many skilled IT workers there — right? But ServiceMaster held a job fair one Saturday and over 1,000 people attended. Company representatives talked to them all, invited the best back for second interviews, and two weeks later ServiceMaster had a new IT department. The company is reportedly happy with the new department, whose workers are probably more skilled and more experienced than the IBMers they replaced.

Where, again, is that IT labor shortage? Apparently not in Memphis.

As far as the database-monitoring problem, ServiceMaster hired a company called DBADirect to provide their database support from that high tech hotbed of Florence, KY. The first thing DBADirect did was to install monitoring tools. Remember IBM wasn't really monitoring ServiceMaster's applications and databases. It was not in IBM's "cost case."

How can a company, 1/100,000th the size of IBM, afford to have monitoring? Well, it seems DBADirect has its own monitoring software tools included as part of its service. That allows them to do a consistently good job with less labor. DBADirect does not need to use the cheapest offshore labor to be competitive. They've done what manufacturing companies have been doing for 100-plus years — automating!

A small company like DBADirect cannot afford to have a big problem with one of its customers. A serious outage could put them out of business. They *have* to do the job right and they *know* it. They have made investments in their business, tools, and processes.

For decades the heart of IBM's services business has been **billable hours**. The more bodies it takes to do a job the better. IBM views monitoring and automation tools as value-added, extra-cost options. It never occurred to them to create a better, more profitable service with more tools and fewer people. With good tools and automation the cost of labor becomes less important.

So what's an IBM customer to do?

The only outside power scary enough to get through the self-satisfied skulls of IBM top management is irate IBM customers. A huge threat to revenue is the only way to move IBM in the proper direction. A big enough threat will not only get a swift and positive reaction from Big Blue, it will make things ultimately much better for customers too.

So if you are an IBM Global Services customer, or work for one, here is exactly what to do, down to the letter. Print this out. If necessary, give it to your CEO or CIO and have them hand it personally to your IBM account rep. Give the IBM rep one business day to complete the listed work. **They will fail.** Then go ballistic, open up a can of whoop-ass, and point out that your IBM Service Level Agreement covers all these requirements. Cancel the contract if you feel inclined.

If enough CIOs ask for it, this action will send immediate shock waves through IBM. Once IBM's customers find out how long it takes to get this information and they see what they get, then life will become really interesting. But don't limit this test just to IBM. Give it to any IT service vendor. See how yours stacks up.

Ask your IT outsourcing provider to produce the following:

1) Ask for the names of the people assigned to your account and the number of hours they worked on the account during the preceding month. This alone will lead to a crisis because IBM tends to have "your" workers also service other accounts. Consider calling for an audit of actual hours worked. If the people are based in India, multiply that number by $1,300. Multiply the U.S.A. workers by $7,800. How much are you paying IBM each month? Subtract what you're paying IBM from the cost of labor. What is the difference? If you have projects or work that is not getting done, make IBM an offer to hire your own contractors to do

the work, and then subtract your cost of those contractors from what you're paying IBM. You'll find with local U.S.A. workers you can often get the same job done better, faster, and less expensively than IBM can.

2) Ask for a list of all your servers under their support. That list should include make, model, serial number, purchase date, original and current asset value, processor type and speed, memory, disk storage, host name, IP address, operating system, installed software, and business applications (don't forget versions and product serial numbers of all these). Look at the list if it ever appears. Is the list complete? Are infrastructure and support systems on the list? How long did it take your provider to produce the list? Did they have all this information readily accessible and in one place?

3) Ask for a report on your storage area network (SAN). It should include:

- Illustrations of the major circuits and equipment, and the load on each component. Are there any hot spots?

- How many disks have failed? How quickly were they replaced?

- Is there a cross reference between applications, databases, servers, and storage pools?

4) Ask for a report on the backup for your servers for the last two weeks. Are all servers being backed up? Are all the backups running in the planned time window? Is there ample time left over, or is the operation using every minute of the back-up window? When backup runs on a server there are always files that are open or locked and the backup cannot copy them. Every day the back-up team needs to look at their reports and make sure that files that were missed are backed up. In your examination of the back up reports you should see evidence of this being done. If you spot any potential problems with a server ask for a list of all the files on the server. The list should show the filenames, dates, and if the archive (backup) bit has been flipped.

Is this list complete? How long did it take your provider to produce the report? How often does your provider conduct a data recovery test? If a file is accidentally deleted, how long does it take your provider to recover it? Can your provider perform a "bare metal" restoration? (Bare metal is the recovery of everything, the operating system included onto a blank system.)

5) Request a test of the back-up system. Identify an important

application or server that has at least a few terabytes of data. Ask your provider to perform a full restoration of the server or database, operating system, everything. How long does it take? When you start the application or database, does it work? Do you have data integrity?

6) Ask for a report on the antivirus software on your Windows servers. Is antivirus software running on all your Windows servers? Is it the same (standard) version? Are the virus signature file(s) current? Ask for case information on any recent virus infections. Is this list complete? How long did it take your provider to produce the report? When a virus is detected on a server, how is the alert communicated to your IT provider? How fast do they log the event and act on it?

7) Ask for a report on your network. It should include:

- Illustrations of the major network equipment, including routers, switches, firewalls, etc.

- IP address allocations.

- Internal DNS entries.

- Current routing and firewall rules.

Is this information complete and current? How long did it take your provider to produce this information? Is this information stored in a readily accessible place so that anyone from your IT provider can use it to diagnose problems?

8) Ask for information on your Disaster Recovery (DR) plans. Here is what you want to know: Documentation on a recent DR test, the plan and results—It should show the actual times tasks were started and completed. Problems should be logged. (It is okay for theyre to be some problems. The purpose of the test is to find and fix them, and to build skills so that in a real disaster the team can deal with surprises.) If you need to recover a file or database from backup, can you? Ask for a list of names from the IT provider of the people who worked on the test. Are they permanently assigned to your contract? Or do you get random people from a "pool?" How many people who worked on the test live full time in the same country as your data recovery facility? Did your IT provider fly in an army of offshore support folks for the test? If there were a real disaster how long would it take your IT provider to assemble a team to support your emergency? Ask for a list of your critical applications to be provided and supported in a disaster.

Is the list complete and correct? Is there sufficiently detailed information on each critical application? How much data is involved? Is the data actively sync'd over a network? How often is the sync'ing process checked? What host names and file systems need to be restored? What application skills are needed to start up the applications?

9) Ask for help desk information. Here is what you want to know:

Ask for a report of all the help desk tickets for the last two weeks. Independently ask your company (not your IT provider) for information on known IT problems over the last two weeks. Compare the information from the help desk and your company sources. Pick a few random incidents from the help desk ticket report. How long did it take to discover the problem? How long did it take your IT provider to begin to work on the problem? How long did it take your IT provider to fix the problem? Was the problem really fixed? Is there an active problem prevention program? Is your IT provider examining the reported IT problems and finding ways to reduce the number and frequency of problems? How long did it take your provider to produce this report? Did they have all the help desk ticket information readily accessible to everyone and in one place?

10) Look for evidence of continuous improvement. Repeat this process once a month. Look for changes and improvements, month to month, and over several months. Is the total number of your IT problems being reduced? Is the response time to fix those problems being improved? Is there clear evidence your IT provider has an active and effective, continuous improvement program?

A good IT provider will have the tools to automatically collect this data and will have reports like these readily available. It should be very easy and quick for a good IT provider to produce this information. A key thing to observe is how much time and effort it takes your IT provider to produce this information. If they can't produce it quickly, then they don't have it. If they don't have it they can't be using it to support you. This will lead you to the most important question: Are they doing the work you are paying them for? If this checklist trips up your IT service provider, then it should be perfectly clear that the quality of their service, and how they view you, their customer, is not good enough. **They are sacrificing your service quality for their profit margin.**

Every CTO, CIO, and/or CFO needs to take this chapter seriously. Your IT service provider can cause serious financial damage to your business. Cybercrime is at an all-time high. The risks to your business are huge. You need to be absolutely sure your IT service provider has *your* best interests in mind. You probably should start talking to your peers at other companies or organizations and compare notes. It would be a good idea, too, to review contracts with your IT service provider. Do they have the proper level of legal and financial provisions to protect your business? If they don't, you need to either amend them, or buy a lot of insurance.

Remember, you get what you pay for. Shopping for the lowest cost IT service is often not the best way to manage and protect the business systems of your company. It is, after all, your business, your company, your customers, and your livelihood at risk.

10

THE GINNI PARADOX
OR HOW TO FIX IBM

Two of the most powerful women in American industry are probably IBM CEO Ginni Rometty and General Motors CEO Mary Barra. As this book shows, Rometty has continued to follow the Palmisano playbook at IBM, while Barra just broke a decade-long tradition of secrecy at General Motors to recall 2.6 million faulty cars, and to admit that they should have been recalled years before. Both women take risks, but in this example one is taking a risk on honesty and a new direction, while the other is taking a risk that Sam was right.

Sam wasn't right.

IBM could fail on its present course, or just become irrelevant.

Information Technology is becoming an increasingly commoditized industry. In time, IBM will have to compete on volume, quality, and cost. This is not something IBM has historically done well. The days of offering unique products and services at a premium price are coming to an end. For IBM to excel in the long term it must adapt to the changing market.

In this chapter, I will explore IBM's current challenges and what I think it should do before it's too late. These are my ideas for what Ginni Rometty should do as CEO.

IBM's business plan today is to reach the $20 EPS by 2015. The executive incentive programs are based almost entirely on short-term net income and long term operating EPS. Incentive programs have a powerful influence on the decision-making process in any company. At IBM it is causing them to choke their existing core businesses and gamble on a few big ideas to make big bucks in the near future. What if these big buck ideas don't work? Where does that leave IBM? Let's look at each of IBM's existing businesses and their big ideas for the future.

THE HARDWARE PROBLEM:

IBM's hardware business has struggled the most recently, and turned in a big loss in 2013. Its difficulties are a direct result of Moore's Law. Moore's Law says that we expect technology to double in capability about every 18 months. There are many ways to spin this law, but the important one is from the customer's perspective. The customer expects to get twice the value from the same amount of money every 18 months. The Intel world has generally followed this curve. IBM has been slower. IBM has focused on making BIG systems that can do a lot of work. These systems are significant engineering accomplishments. The problem is that the Intel world is catching up and will soon overtake these BIG systems.

Over the last 15 years, new technology has been developed to make many computers operate as one. This is the technology you will find in the data centers of Google, Yahoo, and Facebook. With such unified computing we will soon be able to build systems to replace IBM's greatest mainframes for a fraction of the cost. The technology called Hadoop has application to storage and other elements of IBM's hardware business. Soon IBM's unique or proprietary technology will not be enough for it to compete in the marketplace. Computer technology is becoming more of a commodity, and IBM must learn to become a commodity supplier.

THE HARDWARE SOLUTION:

IBM needs to retain and grow its hardware division. The immediate goal should be to return it to break-even performance without any more staff cuts. Next, it needs to realign the business to better serve the market for the next decade. Intel systems have set a benchmark for price and performance, but all IBM systems must get to this level including the i-Series, p-Series, and z-Series product lines. It is interesting to note that the i-Series, p-Series, and z-Series systems all now run on the same processor technology—IBM's Power Chips. It is time IBM had a single unified system design that is highly scalable.

Computing hardware is becoming a commodity. With a single system design, IBM would gain advantages of mass production. With Hadoop technology it will soon be possible to make a system with mainframe capabilities from commodity Intel hardware. IBM should port its i-Series, p-Series, and z-Series onto a unified Hadoop-based Intel computing platform.

Unfortunately IBM is poised to sell its Intel server unit to Lenovo. As I've said, that sale would be a mistake. The important question IBM should be asking itself is: Couldn't we do what Lenovo will be doing? IBM's sale of the x-Series group is more than a financial transaction to get rid of an underperforming business; it is a clear demonstration IBM has not been able to adapt its way of doing business to a commodity market.

I see the x-Series as the canary in the coalmine. If IBM does not change the way it operates its hardware business, then, as the x-series business went, so will go the other systems businesses.

Hadoop technology is setting new levels of price and performance for data storage. This will change IT customer expectations and IBM must adjust. All of IBM's storage products need to become price competitive with the new open systems technology, become easier to set up and support, and take less labor to manage. IBM has access to all the technology needed to make best of class, low cost storage products. They just need to do it.

Imagine coupling a Hadoop storage system with IBM's Tivoli Storage Manager (TSM). You'd create a back-up and recovery system that everyone would want. If they make a back-up product that has the full capabilities of TSM and Hadoop, customers will notice. In saying this I realize that I just gave Symantec's NetBackup product team a great idea. Now IBM should do it first. If they don't it will be another opportunity missed.

IBM recently announced Linux support on some of its power systems. Now it's time to port AIX (IBM's version of Unix) onto Intel. With a growing cyber security problem I believe there is a big market for a secure, well-supported Unix operating system on Intel. The marketplace is still in shock from the cyber-attack against Target stores. There is a need for a super-secure operating system that is as impenetrable as possible. That operating system could be AIX.

THE SOFTWARE PROBLEM:

IBM's software business was one of its brighter stars in 2013. It enjoyed sales growth and good profit margins. The problem is IBM's software business is far from where it needs to be. To understand IBM's situation in software, look at Oracle. For years Oracle was a database company. Today Oracle is much more than a database company. It has developed and acquired a portfolio of business software applications. If you want a human resources system or an accounting system you can find it at Oracle. When it comes to software IBM is still very much in the 1970s. They sell the tools their customers need to write their own business applications. If you have a business and want to purchase finished software you can use to run your business, IBM will probably not be your first choice. While IBM's software division is growing nicely, its long-term potential is limited.

Compared to many other software companies, IBM moves like a glacier. While others produce fixes and updates in days or weeks, IBM takes months or more. IBM runs its software business like its other divisions — with huge bureaucracies and management boards. The best software companies are agile and tuned in to the needs of their customers; this is not how IBM operates today. For the software business to succeed IBM needs to make better investments and completely change how they manage their business.

THE SOFTWARE SOLUTION:

IBM needs to learn how to operate a software business. Software needs agility to thrive. Large organizations with large bureaucracies like IBM can quickly kill a software business. For IBM to gain maximum benefit from its investments in software it must manage that business differently. The stories I hear from IBM's recently acquired software companies are troubling. IBM is trying to mold these acquisitions into a culture that is toxic to them.

Software is not a business you can carve into pieces and scatter all over the world. Software works best when there is a short and tight communications link between the customer and product development. Product development needs to understand the needs and directions of the customers; it needs to be empowered to design new products and versions that will increase its value to the market; and it needs to be enabled to produce those products and versions quickly and efficiently. Software companies work best when they have a core set of excellent developers who are dedicated to the business. Randomly picking programmers from an ever-changing pool of talent rarely works well. IBM's current approach has crushed the life from most of the software companies it has purchased.

Another market trend is Software as a Service (SaaS). SaaS could be a big business opportunity for IBM's Cloud, *if* IBM had software that customers wanted to use. IBM should invest more in software and make more software acquisitions. The company just needs to be a lot smarter about its investments.

IBM needs to reach new customers and new markets. Today most of IBM's business comes from a small number of really big companies. For every big company IBM serves, there are 50 not-so-big organizations that need software and services to run their business. *This is the market* the software division needs to serve. This is where IBM needs to be making more and smarter investments in software. Look at the products Oracle acquired with PeopleSoft and J.D.Edwards for a good list of software IBM should have in its product portfolio.

IBM's own software group knows they are the industry laggard in producing product fixes and upgrades. They know their competition is much more agile and efficient. The most important thing IBM can do to improve its software business is to allow each product group to operate as an independent business. Give them more autonomy to manage and operate their business. Give them the resources (including funding) and the freedom to act.

THE SERVICES PROBLEM:

Not long ago IBM's Services divisions were the big money makers in the company. Buying Information Technology is just one step in a long process. There is much more to do to turn a purchase into a service that contributes value to the buyer's business. Lou Gerstner realized this and made Services a juggernaut that served the company well for decades. IBM's Services divisions used to know how to implement technology, to support it well, to manage projects, and to get results. That is not true today.

For the last 10 years, IBM's Services divisions have been subjected to relentless cost reductions, layoffs, massive offshoring of work, and a scary process of dumbing down the talent. The result is an organization that can barely do the basics and has become a huge frustration to its customers. The problems in services are deep and serious. Most of the great processes IBM developed over the years have been lost. The new business process—Engagement, Transition, and Steady State—has become a "throw it over the wall" process. Each step in the process passes on incomplete, often incorrect work and documentation. IBM underprices the work, and then earmarks its profit. What money is left is used to start up and support the account. The

Steady State teams receive tools that don't work, incomplete server lists, little or no documentation, and often less than half of the staff they need to do the job. How can an IBM support team under these circumstances be anything but a disappointment to the customer? They face constant threats, layoffs, low pay, no pay increases, long hours — it's a sweatshop. Problems, incidents, and projects are also handled in this way — thrown over the wall, underfunded, and inadequately staffed. The important point here is to understand why this is happening. This is a choice made by IBM management. IBM has made the decision to run its services business as cheaply as possible, by taking as many shortcuts as possible. Profit always comes first. Everything else is a very distant second priority.

Global Services has damaged IBM's credibility. This, in turn, has hurt IBM's hardware and software businesses. IBM needs Services to help sell its hardware and software. IBM has said it will make a big push for Services to contribute more in sales in 2014. This looks great on paper. The problem is that Services has caused its customers so many problems that those new sales will be very hard to win, and perhaps impossible. Some teams in Services expect to see pay cuts in 2014, with the promise of commission to make up for the loss. They know their customers well enough to know they won't see a penny of commission.

For IBM to be successful in its future businesses, it needs a strong and sound services organization. The corporate culture that is crushing Services is hurting every division of IBM.

THE SERVICES SOLUTION:

IBM's Services Division *was* the company's most important business. If IBM is to grow again, Services must again become IBM's most important business. As goes Services, so goes the whole corporation. The division has been severely neglected for 10 years. Its customers have been severely neglected for the last seven years.

Global Services is horribly inefficient. There is very little automation. The business information systems are poor. IBM has too many people managing the business and each account. Services is in serious need of a business process redesign, and in need of better information systems. This has hurt the business for over ten years. All the business has done has been to replace skilled U.S.A. labor with cheap offshore labor. Management heads should roll.

IBM must make Global Services more efficient, more productive, and more profitable than the competition. Instead of finding more and cheaper bodies to do the work, IBM should be finding ways to make the core businesses work more efficiently. IBM Services needs to embrace *quality*. IBM should be striving to beat customer expectations, instead of sticking to the letter of the contract and then smugly under-delivering.

When you embrace quality and invest in tools that improve productivity you can do more work with fewer people. IBM should manage most of its accounts with one or two leaders. The small army of Delivery Program Executives, Service Delivery Managers, Financial Analysts, and support staff are unnecessary. The people who run Global Services today do not know what to do, or how to do it. The political environment has crushed innovation. This division could again be the cash engine of the corporation if it was managed better, and if modest investments were made in the business. Investment doesn't mean buying expensive tools that may not work. The inexpensive open source software I use to run my website is vastly better than the collaboration tools used in Services today.

Every good server admin on the planet knows how to write scripts to automate common tasks. It is amazing that even today it takes IBM 40 to 60 hours to fully install and secure an operating system on a server. Global Services should launch a division-wide continuous quality improvement program. Teams should be empowered to find and act on ways to automate the business.

If IBM can invest $1.2 billion in the Cloud, why can't it invest $200 million in Global Services? A wise investment could cut in half the number of people needed to manage IBM's accounts. It could allow IBM support teams to operate proactively instead of reactively. The client experience would be greatly improved, with fewer problems, and things generally running better. If IBM's Services customers were happy, business retention would be better, and more products and services could be sold.

Most importantly, IBM's new businesses would have a strong resource to help deploy and support their products and services.

If IBM doesn't invest in Services, if it doesn't embrace quality, some other company will.

THE CLOUD PROBLEM:

Cloud computing is one of IBM's gambles to find its *next big thing*. Cloud means different things to different people, but what is important for IBM is to understand the business reasons behind the Cloud. It is part of an evolutionary process to reduce the cost of computing. This means less expensive computing for customers and lower profit margins for IBM. It means reduced hardware sales. It implies there will be reduced support costs from Services, too. Cloud means lots of customers, small accounts, low revenue and probably low profit. This is the opposite of what IBM is now telling itself about the Cloud.

What will make or break IBM's Cloud business is Services. Today, if there is a simple server problem it takes four-six people in IBM to fix it. The hardware people don't understand the operating system; the operating system people don't understand networking; the network people don't understand the hardware; and nobody understands the applications. When there is a problem several people with extremely narrow understandings of the environment are put together to fix it. No one has the full picture (called *end-to-end* in IBM-speak). The more parts that are involved, the longer and harder it becomes to fix the problem. When things take too long and get too desperate, IBM brings in its smart people (Architects and Senior Technical Staff Members) to save the day.

The infrastructure used to provide a Cloud service is much more complex than that of a typical IBM outsourcing account. IBM's approach of throwing lots of bodies with narrow skills at the problem won't work with Cloud technology. To support the Cloud well, IBM needs experienced support personnel with deep and diverse skills—just the type of people IBM had 10 years ago and laid off.

THE CLOUD SOLUTION:

In the early days of IBM's Cloud services the designs had shortcomings. Fortunately, IBM bought SoftLayer, a company that knows what it is doing in the Cloud. SoftLayer has a cost effective automated design. Even better, IBM seems to be resisting the temptation to IBM-icate SoftLayer. They are leaving the business and its leadership pretty much intact. This is amazing, and a very good thing. Beyond leaving SoftLayer alone, what IBM needs to do to be successful with its Cloud investments is to fix other parts of the company. Cloud by itself is not enough. IBM has a fighting chance to be profitable with Cloud, but the big question is "how much can IBM really make?"

IBM needs to provide value-added services to its Cloud platform to increase both revenue and profit. There isn't enough money in Platform as a Service (PaaS) for IBM to get a good return on its $1.2 billion investment. IBM needs to provide Software as a Service (SaaS), and to do that IBM needs to have software applications that the market needs. This market is not comprised of IBM's huge legacy customers; it is the other 80 percent of the market, consisting of not-so-big companies that IBM has served poorly (if at all) in recent years. IBM will be selling its Cloud services to this new market, and IBM needs to invest in the software those new customers will want to use.

THE ANALYTICS PROBLEM:

Analytics is another of IBM's investments slated to make big bucks in the future. IBM has purchased several data analysis companies and is now turning its Watson technology into an analytics service. This is a huge gamble. Success or failure in analytics will come down to price and results, and for IBM that's a big problem.

The analytics process starts by building a really big database and copying most customer business data into it. Queries and analysis programs are then run against that data to develop a deeper understanding of the business. Through this process, patterns and trends emerge that were unknown before, information that can lead to business opportunities and improvements. This is not a deterministic process. It involves a lot of trial and error, some guessing, and often some luck. To do the job well it is best to have people who understand the customer's business and industry and are technically astute. Generally these people work directly for the customer.

The costs of the hardware and software for a Big Data analytics project can be enormous. IBM has hopes to make this a service they can offer in the Cloud. That will involve copying most of business data to a database outside the company. Data security is a very serious problem and there are many new government rules and regulations to consider. The next challenge to a Cloud service is TIME—simple math and physics. We're talking about huge amounts of data that may take weeks just to move across the network.

It may be easier and cheaper for companies to build their own Big Data databases in their own data centers. The right path will be decided by the Return on Investment (ROI). Doing ROI analysis from the customer and market point of view is not something IBM does well, or at all. IBM rarely starts a business from the customer's perspective. IBM is more of a "If you build it, they will come—and pay any price" type of company. But will they come? Nobody knows.

THE ANALYTICS SOLUTION:

For IBM's Analytics business to be successful it must carefully balance price with real quantifiable benefits. For the customer, this service must be a good return on investment. IBM has always been very good at telling its customers how good something will be, but promises only work for a short time. Results, or the lack of them, will determine the success or failure of this business.

Many industry experts believe the best way for a company to exploit analytics technology is to build their own Big Data database and train their own people to analyze it. To hedge its bets, this is a service IBM should provide—a turnkey analytics platform, with education and coaching services. Alas, IBM's Pure Hadoop system is neither as scalable nor as price competitive as other industry products. IBM needs a better and cheaper analytics platform.

Now consider IBM's Watson technology. The best computer systems are the ones developed from really good human processes. For a really good human process a company would hire a really good consultant. That person would know what questions to ask, what data to analyze, etc. That information would then be compared with other companies in the industry, and against best practices. The parts of the business needing improvement would be identified. The benefit to the customer would be easily quantifiable. For Watson to work well it will need a lot of business data on the industries IBM hopes to help. To be successful, IBM will have to become a lot better at identifying and gathering that data.

Alas, I fear that in analytics IBM is too little, too late. This is a service mostly for big companies. Most of the big companies who can really use this stuff are already doing it. Analytics at this point for IBM is a one percent business -- only one percent of IBM's customers will have a real interest in this -- and most of them have their own solutions. There is exciting work to be done in analytics; I just don't see IBM positioned to grab a leadership role. There's no way they'll achieve their stated goal of making billions from this business.

THE MOBILE PROBLEM:

IBM invented the first smart phone (the Simon) in 1993. Today IBM is completely non-existent in the mobile market. Apple and Google are the leaders, although Microsoft has been working very hard and making enormous investments to get a foothold in this market. That said, Microsoft is light years ahead of IBM. IBM has completely missed the biggest change in Information Technology in a decade.

THE MOBILE SOLUTION:

IBM cannot buy its way into the mobile market. If it isn't working for Microsoft, it won't work for IBM. Then again, IBM does not have to make big acquisitions to become a big player; IBM just

needs to think differently. IBM should start by looking at the App Stores of Apple and Google where they will find tens of thousands of applications, most of them written by individuals and small companies. This can be an archetype for a whole new IBM behavior — creativity. IBM needs its vast workforce to come up with ideas, act on them, and produce mobile applications. IBM should have its own App Store, which would offer customers a way to learn how to use the new mobile platforms. It could provide a way for the application developers to interact with IBM's customers. Over time IBM could learn and develop mobile technology that is useful to IBM's customers. This is a market where seeing and using a live application is much better than some marketing copy in a sales presentation.

+ IBM should start by partnering with Apple, Google, and yes — Microsoft. There should be no favorites.

+ IBM should purchase enterprise licenses for the development tools for every mobile platform. These tools should be made available to any employee with an interest in developing a mobile application.

+ IBM should make it easy for employees to get mobile devices, especially tablets. Through its partnerships, it should be able to negotiate discounted pricing for them. IBM should pay a percentage of the cost. Half would be nice, but in some world areas, IBM's employees could not afford the other half.

+ IBM should provide internal infrastructure — servers, applications, etc. with which to develop and demonstrate mobile computing.

It's a good plan, though it's probably too late for IBM to be a producer of mobile products. But it must be able to support them. In a few years mobile products will be major part of the Information Systems IBM will build and support for every customer. Most mobile devices are less of a computing platform and more of a presentation tool. Privacy and security is a concern and soon will become a big problem. The better IBM understands mobile technology; the sooner and better IBM can support its customers. There is a place in the market for IBM. It must make up for lost time and become everyone's trusted partner.

QUALITY:

The best definition of quality is "delighting the customer." What do customers want from their IT provider? They want to be delighted with great products and services. They want to love their prices. Quality means being able to do the same thing tomorrow, better, faster, *and* cheaper. Quality is continuous improvement.

It is possible to improve quality and at the same time reduce labor and costs. The companies that mastered this skill went on to dominate their markets. Quality is a culture, an obsession. It must start from the top and involve everyone, including IBM's executives, all levels of management, employees, suppliers, and even customers.

IBM's "Client Experience" (or whatever it is called this week) is a start, but it is not being done right. Yes, you can apply quality improvement techniques to fix a problem. The great opportunity is to fix the *cause* of the problem. In most cases, a poor corporate culture delivers decisions that cause quality problems. IBM needs to change its culture and its values. That starts from the top and must be the highest priority for the corporation. One of IBM's competitors will eventually implement a serious Continuous Quality Improvement program. When that happens, IBM will be toast. History has shown that when a company trashes its quality, neglects its customers, and makes earnings its only priority—bad things happen. Over the last 50 years, the U.S.A has lost many industries this way. If IBM's competitors read this book, it will be only a matter of time...

RESTORE RESPECT:

As of May 2014, "Respect for the individual" is dead at IBM. So is "Superlative customer service." Every decision made by IBM in the last five years has been designed to find ways to spend nothing, do as little as possible, and get to $20 EPS. IBM's vast workforce is operating in survival mode. They have no voice, no means to make IBM better, and they are certainly not going to stick their necks out. IBM is squandering its greatest resource and most of its best minds. Most of IBM's businesses are declining. As business declines, IBM cuts staff. Quality and services get worse and business declines even more. Execution gets worse. Every day customers trust and respect IBM less. They buy less. IBM needs to break this cycle of insanity.

IBM needs to stop taking resource actions against its workforce. IBM needs to start treating its workforce with respect, and as valued members of the corporation. IBM needs to invest in its people and get them working *for* the company again. What IBM is doing today is not sustainable; it is damaging IBM's reputation and brand value. It puts all of IBM's investments in future business at risk. IBM needs its new lines of business to start producing significant amounts of income in the next couple years. It cannot afford to wait until then to fix its support capabilities.

ENTREPRENEURISM:

"Good ideas don't come out of IBM Research; they escape," said Lou Gerstner. IBM has plenty of smart people but many of them are not in research or in leadership positions. Many of these unnoticed geniuses could put IBM's STSM's (Senior Technical Staff Members) and DE's (Distinguished Engineers) to shame, yet they've never been allowed to contribute to the company. Inside IBM there are many great ideas and the know-how to improve every business, but IBM culture is suppressing it. IBM needs to change and help those great ideas become valuable assets to the business. Good ideas should be recognized and acted upon. The gauntlet of opposition to change and creativity must be reduced.

Thirty years ago, IBM was falling behind the market and decided to create its Entry Systems Division. In a very short time (for IBM) the first IBM PC was developed and brought to market. The division was successful because it did not have to follow the rules of the corporation. Today IBM has a very similar problem and the vast majority of the company is simply unable to act. This begs the question: are all those rules and methods by which IBM manages its business really working?

If you compare IBM to its competitors you will find some striking differences in how they operate. Low-level managers at IBM have no spending authority, no budgets to manage, and, in fact, no knowledge of the budget. IBM's managers are not trusted to make business decisions for IBM. I could write another entire book on how IBM manages its business. **My point is simple; no one on the planet manages his or her business like IBM does. And that is *the* problem.**

Near the end of John Akers' time as CEO, IBM seriously considered breaking up the company into several independent businesses. At the core of this was a good idea: IBM's divisions needed to operate more effectively. They needed to adapt to the needs of the market, but the corporate management structure was preventing this from happening. This was the exact problem Lou Gerstner found and fixed when he joined IBM. Well, Lou is gone and IBM has reverted back to its old bad habits.

A NEW BUSINESS MODEL:

IBM has never been the low-cost provider of anything, yet a company of IBM's size and talent should be able to be the undisputed lowest cost, highest volume supplier in the industry. A new way of thinking should infiltrate every corner of IBM. Every line of business should be asking itself: How can we become the best, cheapest, biggest supplier? Every line of business should have well-reasoned plans, funding to act on those plans, and a green light to proceed.

For this to happen, IBM needs to learn ROI thinking. IBM spends far too much on gold-plating new products and services. IBM gives preference to its more expensive proprietary technology over commodity industry technology every time. Good design and good engineering makes the best use of money. If the commodity stuff works and is the best economic choice, then use it.

The billable hours mindset has no place in a commodity market. That is where the industry is going, and IBM needs to lose its billable hours mindset. Instead of perverting the Lean process, IBM should have gone through the time and effort to find out how and why the real Lean works. IBM needs to provide products and services that require little or no support. The fewer people needed to support a product or service, the better. IBM should invest more into the development of its products and services, and eliminate the issues that require people to support it.

A BETTER BUSINESS GOAL:

For a small fraction of its investment in Cloud and Analytics, IBM could bring its existing businesses back to health. It is better to improve revenue and make a profit than to buy back stock to boost EPS.

Twenty years ago, Lou Gerstner brought new values and advice to IBM. These values, as listed in Gerstner's book, are as important today as they were then:

- I manage by principle, not procedure.

- The marketplace dictates everything we should do.

- I'm a big believer in quality, strong competitive strategies and plans, teamwork, payoff for performance, and ethical responsibility.

- I look for people who work to solve problems and help colleagues. I sack politicians.

- (His brother suggested...) Publicly crucify shortsighted proposals, turf battles, and backstabbing. This may seem obvious, but these are an art form at IBM.

- I am heavily involved in strategy; the rest is yours to implement. Just keep me informed in an informal way. Don't hide bad information—I hate surprises. Don't try to blow things by me. Solve problems laterally; don't keep bringing them up the line.

- Move fast. If we make mistakes, let them be because we are too fast rather than too slow.

- Hierarchy means very little to me. Let's put together in meetings the people who can help solve a problem, regardless of position. Reduce committees and meetings to a minimum. No committee decision-making. Let's have lots of candid, straightforward communications.

- We would redefine IBM and its priorities starting with the customer.

- We would give our laboratories free rein and deliver open, distributed, user-based solutions.

- We would recommit to quality, be easier to work with, and re-establish a leadership position (but not the old dominance) in the industry.

- Everything at IBM would begin with listening to our customers, and delivering the performance they expected.

Do you see any financial goals on this list? Lou inherited a financial disaster and made the tough decisions to stabilize the company. His financial decisions were not the ends they were the means. The long-term goal was to align IBM with its customers and the market. That needs to be done again. Financial goals alone will not guarantee success to IBM, and will more likely result in failure.

Afterword

WHAT IF GINNI DOESN'T LISTEN?

Here's what the IBM insider I quoted in my introduction says is coming today from Ginni Rometty's office:

"Ginni is betting the farm on PureSystems. She is also betting the farm on Cloud. The problem is she is blaming flagging hardware sales on Cloud-ification. The problem with that is: 1) Cloud has not become that disruptive (yet), and; 2) Cloud only changes where the demand for horsepower goes, not the demand in total. There is some delta from increased efficiencies, but it's not enough and the change has not been fast enough to be killing hardware sales. Remember it's the hardware sales six months ago that are causing pain; current sales are not yet realized. Basically she is in denial.

"P-series is too expensive. Selling off X-series was stupid. She could have grabbed that market and dominated it. All that was necessary was to act like it's a commodity. 'Hey you can have the IBM logo — cheap!' but she blew that.

"There is no clear strategy; just a lot of high hopes, and secrecy.

"There are some things that can happen now. TATA (Tata Consultancy Services, an IT services company and one-time partner of IBM) can buy Integrated Technology Services and take Services. The selloff can continue until IBM is left only a shell that would in essence be a cross-brand OEM dealership. They can rebrand Cloud offerings and sell IBM cloud.

"Shit, I'm not sure where it's going. It's like watching a cockroach meander across the floor. There is no strategy and no direction. It is almost as though Ginni says, 'Let's turn this corner and see what happens next.'"

Though I requested an interview with IBM CEO Ginni Rometty for this book, she could not find time to speak with me.

COMMENTS FROM READERS ON CRINGELY BLOGS FROM 2007-2013

(Edited for punctuation, spelling and brevity)

COMMENTS FROM 2007

IBM 'top-heavy' with management

I have been with IBM Global Services for over 15 years, and I fear my "value" will come to an end not for any lack of skill or contribution on my part, but solely due to the myopic drive by the executives to make Wall Street happy, thereby maximizing their own net worth due to the enormous number of shares they all own.

One internal rumor regarding Lean was that the external consultancy hired to actually perform the analysis was discharged after their principal finding was that IBM is far too top heavy in the executive and management ranks. Not having heard the answer they thought they were paying for, the executives subsequently took ownership of Lean to pursue the path they had already planned.

Once again, those guilty of plundering and wrecking a formerly great company will retire to a continued life of wealth and ease just about the time the remaining shell implodes.

Anonymous IGS Employee | May 04, 2007 | 12:58PM

Management 'disconnected'

The point that the author is making is that IBM is fundamentally suffering from really bad management, which is not something that can be fixed by Lean, reducing costs, layoffs, etc. As a former IBMer, I saw the quality and rationality of management fall off the cliff after 2002. By the time I left, there seemed to be no vision, or even rational planning about where the business was going. Important work was devalued, nonsense work was deemed "important", plans changed monthly, projects canceled, restarted, and canceled again. There are still plenty of great people and products there, but they are being systematically managed into the ground. Management appeared to live in its own world, completely disconnected from either business or technical reality. Perhaps some jobs do need to be done by cheaper labor pools, but that will not fix the basic problem. Unless they fix their management problems and soon, their days are numbered.

T. | May 04, 2007 | 1:32PM

Feds should fight exploitation

I am currently an employee at IBM. The rumors are true and IBM is laying off a ton of people. They are also telling us to not notify our customers and to continue taking on work. I am not sure how long we all can put up with this. I am wondering why someone doesn't step in, namely our government, to prevent offshoring exploits of this type. It is destroying our society and putting many people on the street to look for a job in which there is a glut of those already seeking employment. I have been notified of another huge cut coming in a month that will be much larger than the previous one and I will most likely be part of that. Wonder why there is a huge upswing in foreclosures? This is one reason. Lives are being destroyed here. Come on politicians, step up and help those that put you in office, or soon they will come to remove you.

IBM in Boulder CO | May 04, 2007 | 3:12PM

Have taken 'bullets' for IBM

I've been an IGS employee for almost 11 years. When they called on me to innovate, I innovated. When they called on me to listen harder to customers, I listened. When they called on me to improve my processes, I improved them, as far as my management - none of who have ever done my job - would let me. When they called on me to broaden my skills, I broadened them. When they called on me to think outside the box, I thought outside the box.

I have taken bullets for this company, its shifting corporate priorities and its thick strata of obscenely overpaid senior management for years. The stock price is up. We had a solid '06, and a good Q1 '07. My division made money last year.

I missed the axe this time - some longtime and fantastically gifted and hard-working colleagues did not. But most of us knew this was just the beginning.

I just bought a new truck. And now I'll be losing my job. At just about 50, my prospects for matching my current income, fairly modest by IBM standards, are dim. I could lose my house. I hope the Darwinian capitalists out there are happy. Enjoy while you can - you're probably next.

Another IBM Employee | May 04, 2007 | 3:14PM

Former customer: IGS is dysfunctional

As a former customer of IBM Global Services, and one that started with them back before they started underbidding everything, I have to say that I don't think IBM could do _anything_ to make IGS better. The individuals I dealt with there were mostly bright enough, they worked very hard, and they genuinely wanted to solve my problems. But they just couldn't, not once, do the job right the first time, as requested.

Disk arrays took three tries to build correctly. Implementations of their own products according to their own plans were never on time -- often by months. When the final delivery came, late, it was usually wrong. Documentation was frequently riddled with errors, and in some cases, wrong in ways such that the machines couldn't have worked if configured as documented. That was ok, though, because the documents had nothing to do with the machines anyway -- there was nothing resembling regular checking that the docs and systems looked like each other.

Most of this was due to management mistakes and big problems with the IBM culture. IGS was organized into teams that looked really good on a management chart, but that didn't work in fact. For instance, the "firewall" and "switch" teams reported to different bosses. You can imagine what troubleshooting anything was like: meetings involving 8 or 12 people, including all the managers, most of whom hadn't a clue what we were talking about. The rest of them were busy blaming the other team for the problem. And all of this was tied up in bureaucratic procedures that would have made Kafka weep. Every mistake led to outages that translated into lost business or SLA payments for me.

I don't see how shipping all the jobs offshore could make any difference: this is a group that just can't do its job at the price agreed to in the contracts, if my experience is any indication at all. It seems to me that, if IBM has decided to milk a few more years of contract payments out of their customers, paying less in salary and pensions is a perfectly sensible thing to do. As Bob pointed out in the previous set of articles on IGS, the customer started getting the shaft long ago. My guess is that very few will still be around once the current contracts all expire.

Acowymous Nonherd | May 04, 2007 | 3:56PM

'Good-bye Big Blue'

I have worked for IBM Global Services (IGS) for 10 years (ISSC before that). Read Jim Collins book, Good to Great. Although this book is several years old, it is still poignant. This book outlines a very detailed study of how a good company becomes a great company. IBM is actually doing everything wrong, almost exactly the opposite of what they (we) should be doing to attain greatness. I have witnessed the decline of IBM, almost like a patient with a terminal illness, dragging on for year to its ultimate demise. Although I have been told I am "protected" (something that I really no longer believe), I have started to look for work outside IBM before a true disaster unfolds. Good-bye BIG BLUE.

Diminished Blue | May 04, 2007 | 4:15PM

IBM's 'contempt' for customers

Lean came through this week and we lost several key hard-working employees, some with 30+ years experience. Americans or Asians will not replace them. Instead, the remaining employees will pick up the slack, at least until the fortunate ones, myself included, are able to find a job with someone who cares.

As a good example of IBM's complete disrespect and contempt of their customers, two weeks ago our level one help desk was outsourced to India WITHOUT THE CUSTOMER'S KNOWLEDGE! We were told not to leak the information to them "because they would be upset," as if they would somehow not notice (they have not so far, although the customer's complaint levels have risen dramatically).

A quitting IBMer | May 04, 2007 | 4:26PM

Living on the edge

I work for IBM too. I lost my server and mail admin jobs to outsourcing 4 years ago. Good, engaging, interesting work I enjoyed.

I moved to desk side services with the expectation that hands-on would always be needed there and that I would be reasonably secure. But my peers and I have watched as each new initiative reduces the perceived necessity for our services.

Customers are not saving nearly as much money with us as they may have expected, possibly costs are actually higher now for their IT services as a result. The more specialized account knowledge and experience are lost, the longer it takes to resolve our customer's problems. That means not only more IBM billable hours for customers paying by the hour, but worse, more lost productivity for our customers. That lost productivity is a huge hidden expense that was largely ignored, but believe me, our customers are catching on.

Living in fear of losing my job and health benefits is seriously impacting my wellbeing and job performance. With serious health issues, it is hard to believe I can find a job, which will allow me to immediately resume healthcare benefits without waiting several months to a year to earn this privilege. Last time I was on the job market the wait was six months before I could qualify to receive benefits. So a transition away from IBM to another job with another company looks very scary, not to mention that with so many techs still looking for technical work, it seems likelier and likelier I may have to retrain for a totally new occupation.

This might be fine when I was much younger, but seems much scarier now that I am pushing 50. I already have enough issues on my plate to cause me to feel suicidal, how many more pushes toward the edge should I tolerate?

Scared | May 04, 2007 | 4:56PM

Half of First Line Managers cut

I'm an IBM First Line Manager that was notified on 5/1. IBM's Lean answer to reducing the "heavy management" ranks is to reduce the First Line Managers. In some areas, almost half were cut. They aren't reducing the levels of management, just the management that the employees report to, so they have less time for their employees. The reporting structure from the worker to Sam will be just as deep.

Anonymous IBM employee | May 04, 2007 | 5:22PM

Toyota practices the real Lean

The "Lean" that IBM talks about should NOT be confused with the "lean" approach as practiced by Toyota and taught by many others, including myself. When I implement lean with organizations, we do NOT lay off people as a result of any efficiency improvement. We create new opportunities by letting "extra" people work on continued lean efforts in other departments or we grow the business to create more work. As Jim Womack says, "Lean is about doing more with less, not doing less with lots less (people)."

It's very sad for the IBM employees. I'm sorry you have lousy management. Don't blame this on real Lean, the Toyota Production System.

Mark Graban | May 04, 2007 | 5:35PM

IBM's Lean a 'perversion'

Lean works. Period. What IBM is doing is not lean. It is a perversion given an honorable name to make it appear more honorable. Lean is about removing waste--whether that's scrap, unnecessary motion, or wholly ineffective management.

It's a shame actually. Had IBM really wanted to implement Lean (which, interestingly, is a service they offer their customers), they could have really saved the company. Instead, they're playing taps as the ships sinks lower and lower.

Lean Aficionado | May 04, 2007 | 5:47PM

The secret is out

I'm caught in this, being an IBM employee. We have been told not to let the user know. Now that this secret is out on the Web, I have no idea what management will say about the "secret". The main problem I see is the language barrier. Frankly, I have a terrible time understanding the folks from India. Very polite and have a basic understanding of processing, but they are not even in the ballpark on job knowledge. But, hey, as the article says, if you get a six-month surge in profits, that's the one and only thing that's looked at.

R Maddox | May 04, 2007 | 5:52PM

Survival is at stake

Those of us who work with IBM's China team know how hopelessly inadequate they are. Testers test products without any real product knowledge; developers who don't speak English develop GUI's; and people who can't write a sentence and who do not know the product write the product documentation.

We know where the Big Blue Ship is heading, and we also know that we have about as much chance of surviving as the third class passengers on the Titanic.

The person who said the reason people aren't jumping ship is because we're waiting for a package is exactly right.

IBEAMER | May 04, 2007 | 6:01PM

Labeled a 'rebel'

First let me state, I work IBM Lean every day and have for the past nine months. We were part of the "innovators" at IBM and were on the line when the implementers out of Chicago hired by IBM for $6 million came in to make Lean work at our account. I lived it, breathed it, so I know what I am talking about. I was there for the executive briefings with the fudged-up numbers from the consultants and we were told what to say and when to say it. I was there when we pleaded with the consultants to give us the basis for the numbers they were spouting, I was there when we told them it cannot work in a service organization as it is laid out, I heard the Toyota speech. I made a simple suggestion that we "don't make cars, we provide a service" and was branded the rebel.

As others have stated this is not true Lean, this is a bastardized,

Frankenstein-ized version of something that was brought in and molded to fit the ideas and perceptions the consultants wanted the IBM hierarchy to see and hear. No substantiations or metrics to prove the numbers were ever brought out, and if we asked for them we were ignored. And yet it continues because the people, who signed the contract and the checks to their "friends" at the consulting firm, can never be proven wrong or made to look bad. And those 2nd and 3rd line managers who did found themselves on other accounts or out the door.

As for the layoffs it is 100% true, I am in the middle of it now and have been for a month, daily calls from the bean counters, "give me 20 people we can release", "no give me 30". Now it's all contractors--you provide support but do not work in a billable job and you are gone, now or in the very near future. Regulars will be next on the block, 2nd line and 3rd lines already have been told they are gone, and the knowledge booted out the door is just phenomenal.

JustAnotherIBMer | May 04, 2007 | 6:54PM

Something 'fishy' at IBM

You, Bob, and the reader comments on the inner workings of IBM are so right on the money. IBM USED to be a great place to work. It's been on a steady decline since the dot.com bust.

Morale is at the lowest point I have ever seen. The rationale for getting RA'd [resource-actioned] (fired, laid off, canned) is not done how IBM tells you its done. It's all done by who knows who. If you are "connected" within the teams you're on, it's not likely you'll be hit. They are hitting folks that have PBCs [performance reviews] of 1's and 2+'s over folks that are 3's. The whole PBC process is a joke. Management dictates that there will be so many 1's, 2's and 3's. You, as a manager, have to tag someone with the 3's even if all of your team is performing at a 1 level. Job security and being an "IBMer" is what drove the 2,040 hours we pumped into IBM. Folks were lucky if they ONLY put in 50 hours a week. What was the reward for dedication? A pink slip. This happens while the execs have 100K lunches; yet cancel our holiday pizza party. I do not see the end of where this is going.

As people have mentioned, if you were a client that just got screwed by this Lean effort, would you renew with IBM? The people I am starting to feel real sorry for are the poor saps who will be left holding the bag when all of the layoffs are done. Our workload, for most folks, is crazy now, but just wait. It seems like it's a race to the bottom with Sam at the wheel. I don't see the benefit EXCEPT to break up the company and raid the pension fund. SOMETHING FISHY IS GOING ON AT IBM.

Is there any hope left for IBM? | *May 04, 2007* | *7:35PM*

Unpaid overtime is mandatory

IBM has been 'lean' for a long time. It's been eight years since I've been allowed to order business cards (cost: $10). When I go see a customer, I just claim I 'forgot' my cards. We have been working years on unpaid mandatory overtime (illegal in some states); if we take holiday time, vacation time, or are sick, we must make up that time with billable overtime hours.

Customer satisfaction is still important; we'll bend over backwards make the customer happy. But often there is no time to 'do it right'. Yes, some customers need to be let go because they demand more than what is in the contract, and thus it is not profitable.

We have been offshoring for a long, long time, but in reverse. The U.S. workers have been doing remote work for India, Asia-Pacific and EMEA. Now this is starting to change, often with cultural difficulty.

The good techs are being burned out. There is no longer a reason to work for IBM vs. some other tech company, no longer a place for a career (i.e. lifetime employment), no longer the best benefits. Certainly not competitive pay. And if you have to replace your vacation time with overtime, why bother?

BT | *May 04, 2007* | *7:40PM*

Lean will be a disadvantage on many contracts

As a current IBM employee, I'm working on a very large, very visible SO and GBS contract. My team has already been affected by this initiative as five of the contractors were let go this week. Unfortunately for me, these contractors are pivotal to the success/failure of the current project I'm managing. Simply stated, we're at a critical phase where they are responsible for the bulk of the work. This won't do!

Project Lean is an initiative that is meant to take fewer resources and spread their work across multiple projects by streamlining the processes it takes to support live environments. At a high level where the execs live and work daily, stated this way makes the decision plausible and even sounds like a good idea. Unfortunately however, I've already begun to see the negative fallout from this and it's only been a week!

The impact has been immediate and harsh. The team members I'm losing are absolute professionals and technically sound. Throughout the previous phases of work they have been stellar. So, on a contract that is already on short resources (fixed price), and just a few short weeks from going live, I've lost five people.

1) It is a total moral killer. 2) I'm already building the case for telling the customer that I must move the go-live date. 3) The workload on the existing resources has basically increased by 30%.

This is a team that when fully staffed is probably four to six people short noted by the extra 160 hours above the 40 hours my team members are working (allowed to claim) already. As an MBA in the trenches, I see this thing really hurting IBM in the long run whether or not it turns into a layoff of 150k people. I'm skeptical of this number, but what do I know. This is obviously driven by cost and IBM's ability to competitively bid projects. What most people don't know however is there is a huge amount of overhead in IBM services organization. The corporation sucks up about 32 cents of every dollar generated through billable hours. If IBM were to spin off its Global Services Organization, this overhead would go away, immediately making IBM more competitive without cutting as many people. In fact, IBM would have the money to hire top notch consultants instead of hiring lower skilled, younger, and/or H1B status employees willing to work 70 hours a week for much less money than the people who really know how to do the job. I read in other postings that many people believe this will cause the stock to go up or down based on whatever belief they may have. One thing I do know is that Wall Street is fickle. Of course large revenues usually (not always) lead to higher stock prices. However, smart analysts know to also look at the overall health of the company, including its customer base, and even customer satisfaction. I believe Project Lean on many contracts will be looked at as a disadvantage, especially with higher profile customers whose environments are extremely complex. In fact, on my project now each new person works with a shadow for the first two months before ever touching the production system solely due to its complexity. Only time will tell. But I'll say this. I ain't sticking around long enough to find out.

Blue is fading | May 04, 2007 | 8:35PM

Lean: 'Don't tell customer'

Take it from an insider at IBM Global Services who has been through the Lean process. When Lean started, we were sternly told, "DO NOT TELL THE CUSTOMER". Most of us knew what was going on. Cutting more of the workforce. They don't care how much it affects the customer. It is like they want to lose the contract. I believe they have already gotten rid of 40 percent of the people on this contract. The workload is now to the point that I'm looking for a job elsewhere. I'm sure next will come the shipping of more of the jobs to India. Many from this contract have already gone there. It's amazing how IBM is putting national security in the hands of folks in another country.

ontheinside | May 04, 2007 | 10:31PM

No confidence in management team

I'm an employee in STG and from my informal survey of my cohort (zero to five years in) it seems a huge number of the really bright folks are leaving voluntarily for better opportunities. I think the big problem is there's very little incentive to work at IBM. Awards are gone, bonuses and raises are almost gone too. Having initiative at IBM is like having "sucker" pasted on your forehead. No one works hard, because hard work is rewarded only with more work.

The projects are understaffed and way behind and basically every layer of project management is lying a little to the layer above it. When we had a 5th line manager tell us when he thought the mainframe product was going to ship, the audience (low-level engineers) literally burst out in laughter.

It's unfortunate, but I think there's a widespread loss of confidence in the management team. Ideally this is when the board is supposed to step in and mop things up, but I'm not so naive to believe it will work that way.

STGer | May 05, 2007 | 12:35AM

Employees 'incompetent'

I've been working at IBM STG for over 20 years now and, unfortunately, the sentiments in these comments reflect the current mood at IBM very well. Sure, outsourcing is happening (I find the layoff number of 150k a bit hard to believe, though) but that is not the main problem around here.

The main problem is, to be blunt, the general incompetence of IBM employees. And yes, that includes those here in the U.S. Managers are completely disconnected from their employees or what is actually happening in their departments on a technical level.

Our manager is remote and we have a weekly department call with him on the phone. While he rambles on with trivialities, we have the phone on mute and are joking loudly about his incompetence. Sometimes it makes me sit back, look at it and feel sad for what this place has become.

I personally will try to hang on until retirement. Wish me luck!

IBM Developer | May 05, 2007 | 2:06AM

IBM management has 'lost touch' with reality

This week was unique. I received an email from our location exec praising a colleague for doing a little extra work to promote IBM as a workplace on the Intranet. On the same day this email was sent, the employee had been 'leaned' along with a few of his co-workers showcased in the video. Ironically the video was titled this is Where I Work. Just shows how much management has lost touch with reality.

I'm tempted to create a video myself; I think 'Where have all the good ones gone' would be a great title. Opening shot: The rows of empty cubicles. Cut to IBM executives rubbing their palms together in anticipation of the short-term stock price rally, and then fast-forward to the day IBM shares are trading on the pink sheets.

CorpSlave | May 05, 2007 | 3:36AM

Company favors low-level employees

I'm a 22-year IBM employee who is getting squeezed out his year. I don't really mind though. My job is a dead-end, high stress, and a poorly compensated one. The workload is horrendous and only getting worse. I will not miss working 12-hour days, weekends, holidays, etc. The company seems to favor young, low-level, poorly paid folks who are so hard up for a job, they would do anything asked of them. I wish IBM lots of luck.

supertech | May 05, 2007 | 8:36AM

People in trenches are the ones losing their jobs

This all rings so true it's scary. I've been at IBM for 8 years in a technical (application development) position for external clients. I have NO FEWER than four to five people a day, whose main responsibility it is to track projects via an Excel spreadsheet, pinging me to see the status of this or that problem/issue. These are the people that should be axed, and yet somehow it seems it's the people in the trenches who are losing their jobs. It's mind-numbing how clueless these managers are. Another pet peeve of mine: receiving several notes on a Monday morning congratulating the technical team on another project successfully completed, from MANAGERS I'VE NEVER EVEN HEARD OF AND HAVE NO IDEA WHO I AM OR WHAT I DO. Does this sound familiar to anyone?

ibmtekkie | May 05, 2007 | 9:25AM

Management is 'non-technical'

IBM's problems are not basic capitalistic forces, not an inadequate, expensive or lazy workforce, its problem is *ONLY* really, really, really bad management (people and policies). Management is completely non-technical and clueless, trying to manage a technical business. Managers have *NO* meaningful contact with their people. This starts at the first level and gets worse as you go up. Upper management is also clueless and doesn't understand the business. They have no idea what to do to make things better, so they come out with a series of stupid moves and policies to try to "Fix" things, and invariably make things worse. The evaluation process (PBC) is a perfect synopsis of this dysfunction, but there are so many others, including "LEAN" (as implemented).

If one were charitably inclined, one could say that it isn't management's fault; they are just completely untrained for the job they are supposed to do.

Managers MUST be able to understand the technical details of the projects they manage. S/W managers must be programmers, H/W managers must be designers. Managers must see their people and talk to them everyday, work on problems with their people, be involved with the work. The managers above them must also understand the technical aspects of the business, even if it at a more abstract level (how one piece interacts with another). If you fix this, and stop these recurring pointless layoffs (mandatory attrition), dictated top-down PBC ratings, everything will fix itself. This death-spiral is new (post 2002), we've all seen it start, and it started because of deliberate changes in management people and policies. It can be stopped, but it will have to start at the top.

T. | May 05, 2007 | 11:41AM

No future for Global Services workers

I was a professional hire at IBM about 10 years ago. I was hired for my expertise in quality improvement. After 10 years of showing amazing results, giving briefings to countless managers and execs, and a lot of hard work -- IBM has done nothing with my work. It's been like pounding my head on a wall. In economic terms, productivity improvement means getting more for less. This is a necessary part of a businesses' evolution. IBM has never improved its internal productivity in Global Services and over the past five years we have started paying the price for it.

IBM's business model has been based on billable hours. When there are problems the answer is to throw more people at it. If IBM had been serious about productivity, the company would have never ramped up to 300,000 workers, or less. If IBM had mastered quality improvement, we would be operating at about 150,000 workers. We would have lots of happy customers and more lining up. IBM could be charging a premium for its service -- as the quality of service and market demand would allow it. We would not be fearing the loss of 50,000 or more of our friends and coworkers.

Change is an important part of the life of a business. The laws of economics require change. It is not an option. IBM refused to change and the economic seismic forces started to build. The earthquake is about to hit and thousands of people will be hurt by the inaction of IBM's execs.

Yes, the quality of Global Services is getting pretty bad. Yes, many people are probably being paid too much for lousy service. Please do not judge the workers at the bottom. They are not in a position to make decisions and their suggestions for improvements have been ignored for years. They, more than anyone else, KNOW IBM has been screwing up and they will be the ones that will pay for it. Put the blame where it belongs and if you are in a position to help a few soon-to-be unemployed IBMers, please do so.

Now some important advice. First, understand the people who caused IBM's problems will still be in power next year. EVERYONE: Sell your IBM stock. It is presently at a good high price. If you are a major investor of IBM, look at what has been happening over the last five years. IBM's execs and board of directors should be feeling your displeasure. If you outsource your IT services, think seriously about insourcing. Let me tell you a secret -- a well run, well-managed IT department can always provide its own services for less than IBM or one of its competitors. Good management is the key. Is IT important to your business? If there is a problem do you want it fixed fast? Do you think sending your support work overseas achieves either of these goals? If you work for IBM, think about your future. If you work in services, think seriously about getting out. There is no future for you. Sorry, but its the truth.

10years@IBM | May 05, 2007 | 12:09PM

Layoffs like Soviet Russia

Yeah, I went through that round of lay-offs back in 2002, some 15,000 in Australia where I was. Everyone knew it was happening, but no one knew what was happening, it was all kept very quiet. You'd pick up the phone to ask a question of someone, and discover they were gone. Then the guy at the desk next to you would be called into a meeting and would never return. I swear, it felt like Soviet Russia at times.

GS was fat, very fat, and could easily be trimmed, but that's how they made money back then by over-staffing and over-billing. But the way they treated people has forever left a foul taste in my mouth. I was 1 of 5 left standing of 200 originally in my department, I was the only person left to support my particular system. I realised that I was never going to get redundancy, so I walked before the stress level killed me. It's not like I was getting the training or leave I was entitled to, it just wasn't worth it. Still, those three letters look good on the CV.

John.

Odysseus | May 05, 2007 | 3:15PM

Offshore work takes longer

I was so fed up with IBM (after only two years there) that I quit earlier this year without having another job. I can echo almost every complaint in comments above: 12-hour workday expectations, imbeciles running three-hour conference calls, management's deafness and indifference. And as an employee working on IBM's offshoring efforts, I can assure you that while it might cost half of onshore labor, the same work takes at least twice as long due to various reasons:

Miscommunications and language differences, time zones (India's labor market is so hot that they can't hire people to work nights, at least for the projects I worked on), insufficient information, and a severe amount of workforce turnover and retraining (again, due to the fact that offshore employees can resign and have a dozen job offers that same afternoon). The result? What would be a 5-minute onshore task became a 24-to-36-hour turnaround for offshore. And that's if they both understood what you wanted and did it right. Since our offshore employees don't talk with our customers, guess who takes the heat for incompetent and slow execution?

IBM had the most insular and untrained management I've ever experienced. The physical locations of the varying levels of management only made it worse: I work on the West Coast, my manager worked in Canada, his manager across the country, and his manager in South America. To me, IBM's vision of a "global workplace" was a major contributing factor to its management problems. Information just doesn't move around.

I chose unemployment over IBM, and I can say without a doubt it was the best decision I could have made for my mental and physical health, not to mention my career. My life since leaving IBM has been a breath of fresh air. You have no idea the weight it puts on your back until it is gone. If you are unhappy there, or you get laid off, you might be unprepared for how much your life improves. I was.

Another Ex-IBMer | May 05, 2007 | 4:49PM

Outsourcing 80 percent of work

I left IBM Global Services five weeks ago. I was part of the Lean project. I wasn't losing my job. But with the lack of professionalism with which IBM treated the employees and the customer was too much for me to take.

I just heard that four of my co-workers (25% of the team) were given a 30-day notice this past week. During the Lean phase/training I was in two months ago, our 2nd line manager told one of the staff that she should look for a new job, as it was IBM's goal to outsource 80 percent of our work.

I agree with all of this article except Lean didn't start last week. Initial planning started seven months ago and Phase 4 of Lean started about 3 weeks ago.

It's pretty pathetic what this country is coming to. Senior

Management will do anything to justify their outrageous salaries and bonuses. Unfortunately, this just doesn't relate to IBM.

Robi | May 05, 2007 | 5:11PM

Managers from the bottom up are not technical

IBM management's problem starts with the fact that even at the lowest level, managers understand *nothing* (technically) about the projects they "manage". They usually have either completely non-technical backgrounds or backgrounds which, while technical, are in completely different fields. They are unable to understand if/why something is easy/hard, short/long to do, why it is important or not, what technical relationship it has to other products, what the implications of a certain decision are at a real (technical) level.

And this is at the 1st-level manager rank. It gets rapidly worse in the higher ranks as managers become less technical. This has been somewhat true for a long time, but in 2002-2003 it seemed to rapidly accelerate. Managers also have no contact with their people to speak of. They are completely disconnected from the day-to-day work of their people or the people themselves (they are often remote or sit in a different building), rarely seeing their people. Managers are just paper-pushers who implement the (often bad and short-sighted) policies that come down from above. Despite this, the company is *full* of extremely talented and knowledgeable workers (for the most part). So all hope is not lost, but their salvation would have to start with a radical change in management at all levels. And who would have to decide this? Management.

Richard Steven Hack | May 05, 2007 | 5:32PM

Lack of communication 'deadly'

Richard Hack has almost hit the nail on the head. The problem is related to the fact that shareholders feel that bringing in money managers at the highest levels will ensure income growth and maintain share prices. These managers then make sure that their senior colleagues think the same way, slowly pushing out the people who know why the products are the way the are and that understand the need for structured innovation.

This lack of strategic innovation then leads to a paucity of profitable new products that forces the same management to cut costs to maintain profits, and that means getting rid of people and reducing services that after all are the main way for the market to converse with its suppliers; this reduction in two-way communication is deadly for useful innovation. To put it in a nutshell: fewer and fewer people in large corporations know why customers are actually buying their products and more and more believe it's only the price that decides!

Ken Harris | May 05, 2007 | 6:36PM

Better managers and policies as easy to hire as poor ones

In response to Richard's point: It may be that all corporations are like that to some degree and many are to a large degree.

The point is though that something changed recently (2003) at IBM to make it more dysfunctional. People are upset (I think), not only because their livelihood is being threatened, but also because a perfectly good company is being seemingly deliberately managed into the ground before our very eyes. Management is deliberately making worse choices now than they were in 2001. This is why people are *so* angry. We all understand global economic forces, but those are like the weather, we can't do anything about it (well not much, not quickly). But this relatively recent change for the worse seems calculated or due to criminal stupidity which the directors should remedy asap. If it was so easy to bring in worse managers and policies, why can't better ones be brought in almost as quickly?

My managers were local and technical (or used to be) in my field until late 2002. Then there was a big reorg and all managers in my 3-line org were replaced with technically clueless and mostly remote managers. Then came the layoffs every 6-12 months, then more really bad high-level decisions, then yearly reorgs and manager changes.

T, | May 05, 2007 | 7:16PM

No one in management accepts responsibility

If you want to run a company like Mao ran China, then this plan will work, just like the Cultural Revolution worked (30 million dead). It will be 20 years before the failure is absolutely evident. No one in management will accept responsibility. It will be blamed upon the environment and upon the lazy workers. And IBM's Mao's will live well until their end.

surfingsite | May 05, 2007 | 9:19PM

'IBM's blue is bleeding red'

I work for IBM and all I can say is that actions being taken immediately on my "in the trenches" team perfectly confirm this. I work for ITG/IGS and am a six-year, 1-rated (highest) performer with a $75k salary. I am in the middle of training IBM India people to do my and others' jobs, presumably to allow us to move on to "other, better" opportunities within the company. Sounds like a line from a bad spoof on the Soylent-Green movie to me.

I can't believe how corporate America is really biting on this. If they saw what I see doing the everyday work with all the logistical and other problems making this happen, they would understand. But frankly, as usual, the decision makers don't care until it hits them in the pocket, which I agree will happen and be very painful. Gone are the days of corporate integrity, even from one of the true pioneers of the concept. IBM's blue is bleeding red and when you mix the two you get a very ugly color, near black like IBM's dying corporate heart.

It is tragically funny watching IBM's stock just soar. If only people saw the REAL IBM as I do. In time they will. Honestly I still am keeping hope the big blue monster will wake up and see it is gnawing its own leg off.

An IBMer | May 06, 2007 | 12:20AM

Customer suffers

The problem with the IBM layoffs (Lean in IBM Global Services) is they don't correspond to the needs of the customer. The layoffs are on top of layoffs on top of more layoffs. Our department has already had two layoffs this year. Not to mention the additional layoffs over the last two years. At some point, there is insufficient staff to do the work. And who suffers? The customer suffers. The stockholder gets a short-term bump, but without good customer service, the bump is blip, followed by a stock drop.

Jacob Drock | May 06, 2007 | 12:34AM

IBM bigwigs don't care

My husband worked for a IBM up until a few months ago, and I am so glad he is out of there now. He was overworked and underpaid, and he knew that Lean was on the horizon. He was tired of going to the client without a good explanation as to why their goals were not being met. I feel sorry for all the businesses that will be affected by this change, but the bigwigs at IBM don't care--they never have cared, unless it was a problem that affected their paycheck and bottom line. Shame on all of the golf playing, jet setting SOBs that run the company, for sticking it to the hard working techies at IBM.

Patty R. | May 06, 2007 | 1:14AM

'Pooling resources' a misnomer

I attended the current wave of Lean meetings. It's pretty scary when a simple schmo like me can figure out that Lean is all about offshoring our jobs and NOT "merging synergies to increase our core competencies". When there is talk of "pooling resources"... hellooooo? That means you'll be pooled right out of a job, especially those of you who just laid out your entire list of daily duties in a neat, prioritized list.

another_schmo | May 06, 2007 | 6:59AM

'Just plain tired'

Well, it is happening. IBM is in a death spiral. Another IBM corporate brain has decided that they can offshore the work being done by hardworking American support people. They think we can just do a "brain dump" of our years of experience to our foreign brethren. We have been trying to tell our managers for years about the problems we were faced with, and that there were better ways to do our jobs. All of our suggestions fell on deaf ears while they implemented the most idiotic pet projects you can imagine. When they tried to merge different layers of support by having software support do hardware support and vice versa, they were somehow thinking that the technical workers could learn it overnight just because management told them they had to or they would lose their jobs. We just shook our heads and spent all of our time cleaning up messes that should never have been there in the first place.

Now there is Lean, and again management thinks that offshoring will fix the problem just because they say it will. Well IBM, I am just plain tired. I will sit here and quietly do my job until you tell me to go. I will collect my severance and my pittance of PPA and go on with my life, and I will NOT look for another job in IT. I am 55 and just exhausted with the IT business. Fifty to 70 hours a week has just taken it out of me. Parents raise your children to be good and honest. Raise them to do anything but work for a corporation. America will not die just because a corporation goes down the tube. We will just find another avenue, and hopefully this time it will be with honesty and integrity. I wish everyone who is losing their job the best this world can offer. :-)

just1waiting | May 06, 2007 | 7:58AM

The only one who counts is the shareholder

I just have to put my 2 cents in (darn--just spent my last raise). I've been in mainframe IT for 25 years and over the past 10 years have had to spend a lot of time training two- for-a-buck programmers on basic things I learned when I was 21 years old.

I have nothing against the offshore folks, just corporations that don't understand that they get what they pay for. If they want to run their cars on four out of eight cylinders then good luck getting up the hills!

Many of us here in the US are at fault also. They cut headcount and we go into "keep it between the ditches" mode, and to management it appears that everything is fine because we take pride in our work so as not to cause a business impact to our customers. We put in longer and longer days to accomplish this while we sweep the dirt under the rug.

The software I support has a lot of dirt under rug, which causes it to use much more CPU than it should. Multiply the cost of this out for 365 days and it's probably 10 times what my salary costs. And just one-hour long business impact to my customer can cost the company more than a year of my salary.

My problem is deciding between my work ethic or just taking my hand off the wheel and letting things go in the ditch. The only thing management understands is financial penalties and the customer complaints. Lean does not have any place for innovation, and customer and employee satisfaction. The only one that counts in this equation is the shareholder.

fighting burnout | May 06, 2007 | 11:13AM

'A high-stakes shell game'

IBM has been doing everything wrong for the past 4 years. If non-employee shareholders could see the internal workings of the company they would dump their holdings immediately. All employees with long-term experience are being forced out (because of their pension plan liability and relatively high salaries), and they are being replaced by college hires in the U.S. or low-cost Indian workers. Customers are dropping their contracts because the service is so awful, and IBM has no new products to sell. CEO Sam Palmisano is raising the stock price by selling off profitable bits of the company and playing a high-stakes shell game. It is pretty close to fraud.

Declan | May 06, 2007 | 1:37PM

Most customers will leave the company

IBM is trying to provide metrics by making us in one of the regional command centers track every ticket we do. After one week, the metrics were not what the execs wanted to see, so they've had the metrics tweaked to provide them with better numbers to justify Project Lean. Apparently, we are doing too much work and "gold plating" what we provide to the customer.

Further, some of the changes in the name of Lean have actually resulted in bottlenecks and roadblocks to getting the job down. Apparently taking phone calls keeps us from doing our job even if said calls are part of a SEV 1 issue.

Finally, IBM seems to think that once we stop "gold plating," customers will decide they can't live without the services we were providing and will pay us more money. While there may be an account here or there that does this, I suspect that most won't and will leave the company as soon as their contract is up.

"Lean Target" | May 06, 2007 | 4:29PM

IBM is doing Lean 'wrong'

While Lean itself is a good thing, by ignoring some of the principles and misusing others, IBM is doing a very poor job implementing it. It will be a total failure.

I believe IBM is using Lean as a crowbar to reduce costs by the brute force cutting of the workforce, rather than implementing the principles of Lean to improve efficiency, effectiveness, customer focus and quality that should bring in more business to which existing resources can be applied.

The difference is very much like putting the proverbial cart before the horse. Doing Lean right (the latter approach) is a prescription for growth, doing Lean wrong (the former) is a prescription for mediocrity at best and failure at worst.

One of the principles, load leveling and production flow, done well, can stabilize the workforce rather than subject it to cycles of mass hirings and mass firings to adjust to the amount of work available. This is one thing IBM will totally ignore because part of their strategy is to dump as many high paid older US employees as possible.

Another of the principles is to empower the workforce to cooperatively solve issues. That's not gonna happen in IBM - no group that has power over another wants to give away that power - there are too many groups that tell you it's their way or the highway to justify their existence.

Another principle is to eliminate the waste of adversarial relationships between management and employee, company and suppliers, company and partners, company and customer. Mass layoffs of course, violate this principle, as does chronically reducing benefits, setting unreachable PBC objectives and scrooge-like compensation schemes.

IBM is doing it wrong - McKinsey is making tons of money telling IBM how to do it wrong. McKinsey just promises those 40% cost savings within six months and tells the IBM brass what they want to hear - "cut, cut, cut", even though it will decimate the workforce, hurt customers, demoralize the survivors and break the business.

Meanwhile, the execs suffer no cuts or sacrifices themselves and treat themselves with large bonuses because they were able to cut costs.

IBM is run by a bunch of immoral, unethical, selfish dictators who are above the onerous policies the rest of us must live by. Lean, as they're using it, is just one of their many tools to raise themselves up and put the employees down.

What ever happened to leadership by example?

Frank | May 06, 2007 | 5:03PM

Global economy is destroying middle class

IBM doesn't have a choice. They have two business segments, mainframes and services. And since all the services companies are moving to India, and India itself has up-and-coming services companies that are growing by the day and slowing chipping away at IBM's business, IBM has no other choice but to keep itself from sinking and leveling their playing field with that of their competition. Sorry, but remember all the rhetoric over the years about how this global economy is gonna destroy the American middle class by bringing down wages. Well, that time is almost here. Stay tuned 'cause it will soon arrive en masse.

Nobody | May 06, 2007 | 10:11PM

Drowning in bureaucracy

To those who insist IBM GS is bloated and poor performing and therefore deserving of this... IBM is not bloated by its number of employees, it is drowning in bureaucracy implemented by executives and senior management. Only a few years ago, teams supported customers. A team, under one manager, built the server hardware, loaded the OS, installed the application, and backed up the data, and supported all of it. A small team, with each member having their specialty. But this high functioning system was replaced with a hands-on team for hardware, Wintel team for the OS, a Domino team for the application, a Tivoli team for backups, etc., all under different managers in different locations operating with greater numbers of people and inadequate lanes of communication. It's not the workers, it's the management, from executive on down. A poorly performing system failing to save money, actually doing the opposite.

prufrock | May 06, 2007 | 10:55PM

IBM taking 'big risk'

We are developing a business approach that only goes through the basic motions and is really not able to serve one's customers well. Our customers will not like it and it won't be hard for our competition to provide something better. Last year Global Services contributed 37% of IBM's total pre-tax income. This is a huge business to put at risk. What is not well understood is the contribution by Global Services to the Software Group and System's and Finance Group. They contribute the other 63% of IBM's pre-tax income and if Global Services falters, or if IBM's ability to support its customers falters, IBM's total income could be seriously hurt. This is a HUGE risk IBM is taking.

HelpNot | May 06, 2007 | 11:02PM

IBM board should be skeptical of Palmisano

This is not surprising. Palmisano has been on a continuing cost cutting to prop up profits while his overall strategy continues to sputter. That "strategy" relied on real growth/profits coming from Services, where he cited a $500 billion untapped opportunity in what he called "Business Performance Transformation Services", or BPTS. This promptly made it into all the executive and Investor Relations presentations/discussions a year or so ago and was the central focus for the company's growth and future. Yet, it is no longer referenced at all. The opportunity was imaginary. IBM's capability to capture any that did exist fell short. Of the thousands of consultants IBM brought in with their acquisition of Price Waterhouse (where the billions spent were largely to acquire expertise/relationships -- i.e. people), how many are still with IBM? As they've left and IBMers have filled the void, how has their service quality suffered? People -- such as the Board of Directors -- should be asking such questions before they give Palmisano another bonus package, much less let him execute this current set of actions.

bill | May 07, 2007 | 6:32AM

In practice, Lean won't work

Needless to say, as a current employee of IBM Integrated Technology Delivery (aka Global Services, Strategic Outsourcing), the information in the article, if true (if even partially true), is highly concerning. Unfortunately, I know, since I was contacted by my manager last week to let me know that resource actions were in process, but that I was not affected (once again I survived the spring chopping block), that some of what is in this article is true. If all of it is true, I will not survive the year.

In theory, Lean could address many of the challenges that ITD faces in trying to be more efficient and competitive, especially on smaller accounts, but in practice, it does not appear that these are the real objectives that IBM is trying to reach with this initiative. If we are truly documenting our processes so that we can hand over ALL of our work more easily to our data centers in India, China, Brazil, or wherever, AND we and our customers are not being advised of this, then this becomes very hard for me to participate in.

I want to be a good employee. I want to be a team player. But I do not want to be involved in assisting in the dismantling of my own team without my consent or knowledge. If the intent of Lean is to dismantle and sell off the remains of what used to be Global Services-

Strategic Outsourcing, then so be it. State that that is your intention, and then let folks act accordingly.

I don't have a problem with corporations doing what they need to do to keep their businesses viable. I do have a problem when this includes lying to and manipulating their employees and customers. I can only hope that this is not what is happening in this case.

Another IBMer | May 07, 2007 | 5:02PM

'Sad' to see IBM decline

I have been an IBM employee for 22 years and a manager for 16 of those years. It is sad to see hard working, industrious and faithful employees that have again been considered "pigs for slaughter", while upper management meets deceptive revenue/profit targets to receive their false "90%" at risk compensation. I have seen the decline of self-serving upper management, which continues to take from its employees and line its own pockets to the extent that I've grown ashamed to be known as an IBM employee and manager. Again it saddens me to see such a great company which had tremendous values (Best Customer Service, Respect for the Individual, and Full Employment) being destroyed to the extent that life long IBM employees will now find themselves on Medicare/Medicaid if, if they complete 30 years with the company, while at the same time executive level managers retire with multi-million dollar a year pension plans. Sad!

Bill Moore | May 08, 2007 | 9:16AM

Cut the waste--from the top

What I find fascinating is how IBM equates Lean with job cuts. Having worked in manufacturing for more than 2 decades (where the lean concept came from), the definition, for me, is the elimination of waste manifest by the fanatical implementation of the intuitively obvious.

Considering that IBM has yet to identify the TRUE waste within its ranks (the blind, misdirected management team), and that it has misidentified its most valuable resource as WASTE, the intuitively obvious answer is to cut the waste - from the top - starting with Sam and moving lower through the ranks until you reach the people that actually do the work.

Instead, IBM starts at the bottom and never moves up more than a layer or two.

Sam, when you are finally in the job market, don't call me. You are a waste of time.

The Builder | May 08, 2007 | 9:32AM

I am one of those employees recently affected by this Lean approach, and it is a mean thing that IBM is doing. The reasons that management and the executives have provided make absolutely no sense, and it's all about the bottom line, not the people. IBM has the public fooled in thinking that they care about people and that is so far from the truth.

In my organization alone there were over 70 people affected and we were herded in, told the news, and told to look for internal jobs on your own. What chance do you have when you have 400 other people looking for 30 job openings across CSO Fulfillment. But according to IBM they have satisfied their part of giving you a chance to find a job, how unrealistic, but remember it's not about respect for the individual anymore, it's about making money the cheapest way possible.

Our U.S. customers were already struggling when things moved to Brazil. With the language barrier already a problem, now you're adding two additional countries to the mix. Customer satisfaction does not matter, the primary objective is the bottom line.

Sam and his executive group will walk away set for life without spending one hour with the real customers and employees who made the company what it was, not what it is today because it's not the company that Mr. Watson created in his vision. I'm convinced that he's turned over several times in disgust with what the company has become.

Pendergrass | May 08, 2007 | 10:06AM

Is cutting fat really age discrimination?

IBMers, here is another way to look at the problem. Go to the HR intranet site and run a pension report on yourself. Run it for the years you will be 50, 55, 60, 65... Look at the lump sum value. One of the things you will notice is it will take a big jump in the last 10 years of your career at IBM. What does this mean? It means IBM is waiting until the last minute to fully fund your pension. When you have 150,000 U.S.A. workers this is a HUGE financial liability. Every IBM worker is a liability to the company. If your future value to the company is less than your future pension and healthcare costs, your job will be cut. It is a simple spreadsheet calculation. Companies have been doing this for years. Firms call it "cutting fat" or "becoming more lean". The affected workers can call it age discrimination. When a company underfunds its workers pensions that is usually a good indication they never intended to keep you until retirement. Run your own numbers. See it yourself. For you non-IBMers: What is happening in IBM will probably happen to you too.

10years@ibm | May 08, 2007 | 10:41AM

The high cost of over-delivery

I can only talk about the part of the business that I know. I have never believed that this rush to offshore was inevitable, though once it started, its acceleration certainly seemed to make it that way.

IBM should have broken away from unprofitable customers long ago, certainly as early as 1996 when I joined the company. I think we have suffered from weak management that has been reluctant to remind large customers of the terms of our contracts with them, and so have led us to over-deliver at huge cost.

We have bid teams that go out and chase business and make all sorts of promises that, had they consulted the service delivery and technical personnel tasked with fulfilling these promises, they would have realized were unrealistic. The contract's signed, the bonuses are paid, the untrained, unmotivated staff do their best (but fail) and the financial penalties kick in. We cut staff, the good staff that sees the writing on the wall and leave, and the cheap staff that replaced them can't even deliver what we delivered last year. And so on, and so on...

I can't believe in Lean because it seems already to be adding another level of bureaucracy to an already almost paralyzed organization. It's destroying team spirit because it's putting people in a position where they have to tell colleagues "that's not my job" or "can you put that in writing or fill out form so-and-so?" From what I read now, these are its minor failings.

We've gone too far - none of the initiatives to put a finger on the global pulse will make any difference because so many workers don't think IBM will be a viable player in five to ten years, and they're looking for the door.

11years@ibm | May 08, 2007 | 11:15AM

Lean: Poor execution

Writing as a shamed IBMer watching the train wreck happening: Lean does provide a good model for how IBM Global Services could do business. The problem is in the execution: Pay the consultants big bucks going in, then drop them half-way through the conversion; execute the conversion done in hurry-up mode with no prior thought given to infrastructure; ensure that every team is isolated and will stumble across the same common problems one by one and then invent their own set of solutions which probably won't interface smoothly with any other team's (or management's future requirements); schedule a workforce reduction just as the teams are beginning to build those solutions; schedule week-long mandatory face-to-face team kickoff meetings but only at the last minute so the travel budget is blown on high-dollar airfares; hit the paying customers first instead of IBM's traditional method of tasting our own cooking before laying it on the public table; change the customer interface week-by-week as the teams try to adapt again and again; measure progress solely in terms of resource reduction, dropping all pretense of measuring anything relating to effectiveness or customer satisfaction; chase away customers instead of training the marketing staff to make and hold to good costing decisions. These are all indications of sloppy management by slogan rather than than careful thought. It's not the worker bees that are being paid too much, it's management that is being paid far too well considering the quality of work they've done.

ByteMasher | May 08, 2007 | 1:29PM

Hands tied

IBM can't even perform layoffs right. A friend of mine works in the Lean program, which involves travel to other sites so she can make layoff recommendations (she transferred there to avoid getting laid off herself). However, in an attempt to save money IBM has clamped down on travel and now she can't even go to the site to help figure out who to get rid of.

TennSeven | May 08, 2007 | 2:59PM

COMMENTS FROM 2009

'It's all about executive bonuses.'

IBM does not give a rat's ass about the state of the U.S. economy nor cares about the U.S. workforce, nor the quality of IBM service and products. IBM products and services to the people in the know are way overpriced and are very low on the functionality scale.

IBM does care about stock prices, however. Not for the "shareholder" as is claimed, but for the CEO and upper level management. It's all about executive bonuses and stock options.

When you accept this as it is, which is the truth, then you will understand the rapid and the "damn the torpedoes" attitude about shedding the American workforce. Americans developed the technology IBM is peddling. The Indians and Chinese are copying this technology without understanding it.

I am ashamed to admit I am in IBM management for now, but I will speak my mind until I've located another job.

IBM Manager / August 25, 2009 / 6:15 pm

Free-market capitalism

I've been saying this for years: The theology of free-market capitalism is wonderful for consumers and efficient production of goods and services (perhaps, with caveats), but it sometimes makes incredibly poor social policy, since profits don't respect borders. Now we have companies too large to fail, but also too large to save (Fortis Bank, anyone?), and their sheer size and political throw weight allows them to influence public policy to the detriment of the citizenry. Yet they are surrounded by political allies who are blinkered to the long-term social consequences. I suppose we will have to have an actual full-scale financial or industrial collapse before things can change. Tragic.

Of course part of the problem is government — because politicians are also short-term thinkers, concerned about re-election and the extraordinary costs of campaigning and fundraising. By the way, much of those costs go to television ad time, which benefits (ahem) corporations. We could lower campaign costs by requiring political ads to be a free public service as a condition of licensing the public airwaves. We could also outlaw corporate contributions, period. Otherwise corporations have over scaled influence on the political process, which allows for distorted public policy. And by the way, the benefits of such distortions aren't evenly distributed throughout the corporate world: think tax breaks and subsidies embedded in targeted earmarks that go to a few -- sometimes a single — entity.

Robb Allan / August 25, 2009 / 10:07 pm

The price of stock buy-back

The stock price is everything, but the motivation isn't for the investors. The executives and the board get most of their compensation through options. This is why IBM borrowed more than $30 billion to buy back stock. It reduced supply and increased demand.

Similarly, IBM contracted services has cut staffing so severely that basic commitments can't be met. The costs are reduced, but the contracts remain in place for the time being. Sure the contracts won't be renewed, but that won't be an issue until after many options have been exercised.

In the meantime, IBM's profits are way up while their revenues are down. This cost-cutting model of profit making will run out when there aren't sizable numbers of American jobs to cut. It will be difficult for IBM to pay back the billions of long-term debt that the current executives and board saddled the company with.

Bob / August 26, 2009 / 5:00 pm

IBM a 'disaster'

IBM U.S. is a disaster and working there is enough to drive anyone crazy (literally). Over 10K employees have been fired since January 2009. And the bloodshed is not stopping. More rules and processes are in place to help facilitate the exit to the door faster and faster. And the offshore replacements? They suck.

Sam and company should just move the entire U.S. company to India and be done with it.

Daniel / August 27, 2009 / 4:14 am

Weak CIOs

The real issue is the tragic, and pervasive lack of IT leadership across swathes of corporate America (both private, and governmental). In my opinion, even after getting royally shafted (which is by far the case with most external resource based delivery), weak, and incompetent CIO's keep coming back for more. It appears that providers like IBM know they don't need to fear client backlash from poor delivery (in most cases a well feigned mea-culpa suffices), hence, the license to bluntly cuts costs to meet short-term bonus objectives. It's a case of Dumb, and Dumber, and their incestuous cycle of life that often results in absolutely nothing.

Anonymous Coward II August 27, 2009 at 1:38 pm

Apple creates better products

"I have no idea how IBM can remain ahead of Apple still at #2 with no product or service not replaceable by any decent open source/freeware company, except perhaps by pure brand name and salesmanship."

Yes, it's salesmanship, basically. IBM sells 'enterprise' software. Read what Paul Graham says on IBM and 'enterprise' software.[1]

The problem is that the people who are in charge of choosing and buying 'enterprise' software, that is, CTOs or CIOs of large companies, aren't the same people using the software, that is, the low-level workers. If the workers have trouble using the software, the CIO/CTO doesn't care. He'll just tell them to 'deal with it' or whatever. Of course, bad enterprise software does cause a loss in productivity and a drop in profits, but the link between cause and effect is so diffuse that it's easy to ignore or explain away.

Apple on the other hand sells their products directly to the people who use them (and, I guess, their parents in the case of teenagers). If their products aren't good, people will simply stop buying them.

Another reason why Apple creates better products than IBM is that Apple doesn't mind employing creative oddballs and letting them loose on the things they're good at (which is maybe because they have a CEO who is a bit of a loose cannon himself). Apple is willing to take the bad (i.e., a certain amount of rebelliousness) with the good in hiring creative, intelligent people. This used to be true of IBM in the Seventies and earlier, but is no longer true. To get ahead in today's IBM, with it's Stalinist PBC [performance evaluation] system, it's best not to have too strong of opinions on how to improve the product if those opinions

---

[1] http://www.paulgraham.com/colleges.html

differ from others.

The people who survive and thrive in today's IBM are those who would have survived and thrived as Soviet apparatchiks in Stalinist Russia. I know that sounds like hyperbole and I admit it's not true of everyone who succeeds in IBM, but it is, by and large, the case.

Paul Reiners August 28, 2009 at 4:44 am

Globalism is 'a lie'

You should read Tom Friedman's book "Hot, Flat, and Crowded". He talks about how the current model is about to collapse. Lets face it, globalism has been nothing but a lie. First, they told us don't worry, only menial jobs that nobody wants and don't pay very much will go offshore. We'll get training for those high paying jobs like engineers, scientists and the like. Jobs went offshore, but training didn't materialize. This caused all manufacturing to go overseas, whether to Mexico, China or India to the point where you can't find a single thing that's made in America on the shelves.

Now that they have decimated manufacturing, they are moving those high paying jobs overseas. In a couple of years, the only jobs available to Americans will be slave wages. They have accomplished what they wanted. Which is to reduce America into a two-class system. Either you are rich or you are poor. No middle class. And by the way, whatever class you are born in that's the class you die in. The American dream RIP 2009.

Fed Up with multinationals / September 2, 2009 / 1:51 pm

Globalism: American consumers win

Your grasp of economics is limited at best. As much as you bemoan the loss of a job at IBM for the American IT worker, this is great for American consumers as prices drop from using Indian IT workers. Further, those American IT workers are now freed up to think up the next big thing, from which a bunch of new jobs can spring. If they can't think of anything, they SHOULD either move to India or take a lower-paying service job as that's all they are good for. As for your kids, they'll have a far better life than you ever did, just for being lucky enough to be born later in this time of explosive growth rather than earlier like you.

Ajay August 28, 2009 at 11:01 pm

Indian IT exploits workers

The problem with that argument: The "consumers" of those Indian workers are not American "consumers" but the managers of corporations, who turn the savings into bonuses for themselves. Self-serving arguments tend to be transparent. If Indians were so much better and not just cheaper, India would be employing themselves in support of their domestic corporations. They aren't, of course. Indian IT is simply exploiting other Indians and a corrupt exchange rate system.

Robert Young / August 29, 2009 / 2:45 pm

Moving the Pro's out

IBM once had a strong union presence when it manufactured things – often with nasty chemicals and compounds – that needed a union to enforce good safe working conditions. Now IBM doesn't do so much directly anymore and if anything it is the professional associations that ought to have defended programmers and consultants from management's poor practices.

It's really a shame the ACM and the PMI, the SANS security bodies, etc., haven't spoken out against IBM's policies of internal resource actions aimed at hiring younger less experienced professionals and selling them to customers at the same rate as the experienced ones.

IBM services divisions tend to pack up and move the pro's after the 1st year of a contract, then replace the with semi-pros in the 2nd and by the 3rd year utilize contractors in all possible ways, by the 4th+ your in a matrix of support which means the guy who's caring for your system is working more than several accounts that day you just get this particular guy cause you were next in the global queue. I think IBM has shortened this cycle as well.

IBM was regarded in my generation as a top choice job for R&D. Today it is hoped IBM will just buy our company that others and I fast started with our new technology. We cache out and reform a new company with persons we know and trust. Then IBM system will gut our former tech and water it down and that tech will decay due to no one "owning" the ideas behind the tech in the Global company.

The open secret is that IBM now considers R&D purchasable, technology fungible and its workers dispensable. It has to — else no company will keep buying IBM. It is not so much a question if tech is dispensable or indispensable. No one argues a business can deal without email. It is, "What is an email system of tomorrow, that will aid my company to produce/sell more things? If my IT vendor's workers can't, or aren't allowed the time to learn the new system to support it, they are dispensed with."

The dangerous idea is that many U.S. tech companies are envious of IBM's ability to reach fiscal targets and adopt the same means. This is very dangerous to both the U.S. & Global economies.

turtleshadow / October 18, 2009 / 10:51 am

'What about IBM's vaulted Business Conduct Guidelines?'

A few years ago I attended a charity event. At the event were a VP from IBM and a VP from one of IBM's "partners." The two VP's had a good thing going. They would take turns taking the other on very posh junkets. The "partner" took the IBM VP to the Super bowl, the IBMer took the "partner" to the US Open. I had just finished my annual signing of my Business Conduct Guidelines. It was clear IBM meant "do what I say, not what I do."

I have a very bad feeling about this.

Global Services Survivor / October 19, 2009 / 10:58 am

No top talent anymore

The problem with IBM's offshoring strategy is that IBM is not hiring quality people in those low-cost countries nor paying for top talent. Turnover is high, skills are low to non-existent, and experience is nil. All of which adversely and greatly affect the quality, timeliness and productivity of these global resources.

Poor quality, poor productivity and poor timeliness, combined with immaturity and lack of discipline, mean delivery failures and not just a few. After many resource actions the remaining experienced professionals in high-cost countries are subjected to near sweatshop conditions.

Like several other posters, I'm one of people that come in to pick up the pieces after global resources' incompetence causes mishaps, crashes of other such failures.

The scary thing is that the global resources aren't getting better – their skills aren't improving, they still show poor ownership of issues, they make no effort to teach themselves skills and the maturity issues aren't improving. They still can't handle even the most routine and simple tasks without help. Meanwhile IBM continues to resource- action the experts that keep the joint running.

The sad thing is that the global resources aren't being held accountable for their failures, failures are always blame on their US counterparts. Who is Sam going to blame when there aren't any US professionals left.

The question is how long will it be until the global resources teams can do an acceptable job of service delivery and product development. The follow-up question is whether IBM can survive long enough for the global resource teams to become effective. IBM needs to consider that the bitterness of poor quality will linger in our clients' shops long after the sweetness of meeting the quarter's financial targets.

Frank / October 20, 2009 / 8:33 pm

Questionable principles

Dear IBM Management:

The following is why most of us chose to come to work for IBM. Today it is questionable if the company is living up to any of its principles. If these are no longer the principles of the company, please update them.

1. Respect for the Individual

Our basic belief is respect for the individual, for each person's rights and dignity. It follows from this principle that IBM should:

a. Help employees develop their potential and make the best use of their abilities.

b. Pay and promote on merit.

c. Maintain two-way communications between manager and employee, with opportunity for a fair hearing and equitable settlement of disagreements.

2. Service to the Customer

We are dedicated to giving our customers the best possible service. Our products and services bring profits only to the degree that they serve the customer and satisfy customer needs. This demands that we:

a. Know our customers' needs, and help them anticipate future needs.

b. Help customers use our products and services in the best possible way.

c. Provide superior equipment maintenance and supporting services.

3. Excellence Must Be a Way of Life

We want IBM to be known for its excellence. Therefore, we believe that ever task, in every part of the business, should be performed in a superior manner and to the best of our ability. Nothing should be left to chance in our pursuit of excellence. For example, we must:

a. Lead in new developments.

b. Be aware of advances made by others, better them where we can, or be willing to adopt them whenever they fit our needs.

c. Produce quality products of the most advanced design and at the lowest possible cost.

4. Managers Must Lead Effectively

Our success depends on intelligent and aggressive management, which is sensitive to the need for making, an enthusiastic partner of every individual in the organization. This requires that managers:

a. Provide the kind of leadership that will motivate employees to do their jobs in a superior way.

b. Meet frequently with all their people.

c. Have the courage to question decisions and policies; have the vision to see the needs of the Company as well as the operating unit and department.

d. Plan for the future by keeping an open mind to new ideas, whatever the source.

5. Obligations to Stockholders

IBM has obligations to its stockholders whose capital has created our jobs. These require us to:

a. Take care of the property our stockholders have entrusted to us.

b. Provide an attractive return on invested capital.

c. Exploit opportunities for continuing profitable growth.

6. Fair Deal for the Business Associate

We want to deal fairly and impartially with associates we do business with. Historically, this has meant our suppliers of goods and services. In the current environment, in addition to suppliers, we have a variety of joint ventures, research partners, and third-party channels of distribution, including independent dealers, VAD'S, VAR'S, and OEM contractors. Each of these is a "supplier" of resources, expertise, or technology that we need to move our business forward. And all of these relationships must be managed with the same care and the same ethical concern that we have traditionally pledged our suppliers. Specifically, we should:

a. Select business associates according to the quality of their products, services, or expertise, their general reliability, and competitiveness.

b. Recognize the legitimate interests of both the business associate and IBM when negotiating a contract; administer such contracts in good faith.

c. Avoid having business associates become unduly dependent on IBM.

7. IBM Should Be a Good Corporate Citizen

We accept our responsibilities as a corporate citizen in community, national and world affairs; we serve our interests best when we serve the public interest. We believe that the immediate and long-term public interest is best served by a system of competing enterprises. Therefore, we believe we should compete vigorously, but in a spirit of fair play, with respect for our competitors, and with respect for the law. In communities where IBM facilities are located, we do our utmost to help create an environment in which people want to work and live. We acknowledge our obligation as a business institution to help improve the quality of the society we are part of. In the conduct of all our business activities, IBM takes positive actions to insure equal opportunity to all, without regard to race, color, religion, national origin, age or sex-. It is also our policy to provide employment opportunities to qualified handicapped individuals, disabled veterans and veterans of the Vietnam-era. We want to be in the forefront of those companies, which are working to make our world a better place.

To IBM's Senior Mgmt. / October 21, 2009 / 4:18 am

End of the American empire?

IBM is mean. IBM wasn't nice to me. Blah, Blah Blah. IBM is a global company with global operations. It puts the work where it is best suited. Fat, dumb, low-skilled, overpaid Americans with a massive sense of entitlement don't rank well in the global marketplace. It's just another sign of the end of the American empire.

And spare us the "IBM is about to collapse as layoffs will wreck contract performance!" junk that has been recycled regularly here since about 2003. Aside from whining aforementioned fat, entitled Americans, there is no evidence. Anecdotes are not evidence, corporate results are, and IBM's have been good for at least the last 5 years.

I don't work for IBM, but the pathetic bleating from the ex-IBM worker bees is tiresome. There are 400,000 IBM employees so it can't be hard to find complainers. If you are so terrific, take your payout, and go get another job.

Koptwan Indernaz / October 21, 2009 / 5:58 am

IBM cutting customers short

Wait until your employer kicks you in the head and endangers the financial well being of your home and family. Maybe you'll feel differently. IBM was different. While most companies treat its workers like mindless pawns, IBM chose to respect and value its workforce.

But forget the workers for a minute, there is a bigger issue. A company is as good as its word. If you agree to buy a product or service from a company, you expect to get what you bought. You expect to be treated fairly and honestly.

In most aspects of IBM's business it is cutting its customers short. IBM is promising the world and delivering a lot less. They are not keeping their word, their commitment to their customers. IBM is not treating ANYONE fairly or honesty — its employees, its partners, and its customers. THIS IS THE CORE OF THE PROBLEM.

I have watched scores of friends at IBM get laid off. I can deal with an economic downsizing of the company, making the necessary adjustments in response to business changes. I support 22 customers who believe they are getting 24×7 support with 30- minute response times. The truth is there is no one on staff providing this service. We miss over half of the problems and find out about them when the customer calls. It takes about an hour to get someone, usually overseas assigned to work the problem. They have never worked with the customer before, they know nothing about the customer's applications, and they have never touched the customer's systems before. When a customer pays for 24×7, 30-minute service it is usually because their applications are pretty important to their business and outages can be very expensive. When it takes us 2-4 hours instead of 30 minutes to fix a problem; that is not good.

IBM made commitments to its customers. IBM is reneging on those commitments. IBM expects me to withhold the truth and give the customer the impression we are doing what we promised. IBM expects me to deliver service without the staff or tools, and to lie to my customers. If the customer discovers the truth, I am the person IBM will sacrifice. I am the one who will suffer the consequences. I could lose my job and my livelihood while those who made the decision to cheat my customers are not held accountable.

The fact jobs are being off shored, and pay and benefits are being cut is just one SYMPTOM of a much bigger problem. If these things were being done to adjust to a changing business that would be understandable. What is really happening is a vast culture of deception by the senior management of one of the worlds largest companies.

Ouch / October 21, 2009 / 7:46 am

As an IBMer, I've never seen a budget or a business plan. I don't know what the business strategy is and I don't contribute to its development. When I first started working at IBM I thought this was very unusual. Then I found out 95% of IBMers are kept out of the business information loop. It is IBM culture for its senior management not to tell anyone anything, inside or outside of the company. If you think IBM does some really dumb things and has problems, this is why. How can you expect teamwork and innovation when 95% of the company does not know what the company wants to do, or how it is doing, where it is headed? To IBM leadership it is not necessary for us to know the situation on one of our Senior VP's. In their eyes we're not important enough to merit that courtesy.

How many IBMers have been asked to get their PBCs (performance reviews) done three months early? There is only one reason for this — so that they can have the next resource action sooner.

Followup / October 23, 2009 / 1:17 pm

COMMENTS FROM 2011

Clever Project

I remember reading an article in 1996 about IBM's clever project involving weighted graphs of hyperlinks.

The Clever project seemed like a very interesting piece of research and the Google founders seem to have agreed. Why didn't IBM turn this into a publicly accessible search engine?

Vijay / January 14, 2011 / 2:00 am

IBM thought they could sell search engine

The project actually started a number of years earlier, very close to the time Google was breaking into the market and AltaVista was the preferred search engine.

It was IBM's belief they could search and index the whole Internet, then SELL it as a premium service to companies and universities. It never occurred to IBM management that one could offer such a service for FREE and pay for it with advertising.

IBM's mindset was in the past, firms would be willing to pay a premium for an IBM branded service. Google's mindset was in the future, Internet based services should be free.

IBM saw the effort as a great way to sell lots of hardware. To offer a free service Google had to find a way to deliver it using very low cost, commodity hardware. In doing so Google developed a lot of really great technology — technology that inspired cloud computing and storage.

Maybe there is some truth to the saying "necessity is the mother of invention." Thinking out of the box, thinking towards the future led Google down a very different path. In time IBM realized they had a nice technology that they could not "sell" and now it is a historical curiosity.

John / January 14, 2011 / 12:50 pm

Offshoring doesn't make sense

The whole outsourcing/offshoring thing is a product of economic rationalism triumphing over common sense and experience. Total outsourcing never works because in the vast majority of cases the contractors don't have any ownership of buy-in to the systems they are looking after. They don't have to care. They just have to live up to contractual obligations, and if the customer's lawyers weren't sharp enough, then this can lead to all sorts of problems. And I have seen it happen time and again. As for offshoring – any

One who trusts their systems to this strategy deserves everything they get. From a systems support point of view it quickly gets very difficult. Time zone and language barriers are a reality and impede the support process. Forget your RTOs.

Steve / June 16, 2011 / 1:43 pm

Saying 'yes' means risk

Large companies start answering all questions of "why" with "no". When you are a startup, you don't say "no" to many things, because you have nothing to lose. When you are large, it is a lot easier to say "no", because saying "yes" involves risk, and most people are risk averse. It is that aversion to risk, which leads to phrases like "nobody ever got fired for buying from IBM" (even if IBM's products were, say, below par).

I agree that there is a big part of "what" and "how" that large companies also apply, but those what and how are there in the small companies and startups, too, but again, there is less to lose and the people involved are more likely to take risks."

bojennett December 21, 2011 9:01 am

Apple on the offense

"You are right about the well-documented industrials of the past that go on uncontrolled (albeit slow) death spirals for they could 'a this or should 'a that, but didn't – Digital anyone? U.S. Steel? Western Union on A.G. Bell's invention of the telephone?

All those losers have one thing in common – they were all defensive and not offensive.

Apple, for example, is obviously offensive in nature. They try to out-innovate anyone who tries to get near. Being as offensive as Apple relegates an existing market to obsolescence just when startups and competitors start to catch up. That keeps Apple a generation or two ahead. This will continue to be Apple's engine of growth for as long as the curious, smart, and creative folks in the middle to upper management are heard from and not ignored by the CEO."

Rick Hunter December 21, 2011 at 1:51 pm

Mid-size companies most at risk

"I have been pondering the fate of big companies in an economy of upheaval, disruption and uncertainty. While most are doomed to eventual failure, there is something to be said for size. With sufficient size, a company can buy time. They don't have to be the first mover, they can wait and let nimble start ups serve as their R&D.

In my experience, companies must move through five stages of growth to stay alive:

1. The Entrepreneurial Enterprise (newborn) – characterized by intense customer focus. Driven by a sense of mission. Dominant question is "why?"

2. The Performing Enterprise (toddler) – characterized by emphasis on growth . Driven by performance. Dominant question is "what?". Figuring out its sustainable value proposition and market.

3. The Systematic Enterprise (teenager) – characterized by over-confidence. Driven by repeatability and predictability. Dominant question is "how?"

4. The Adaptive Enterprise (young adult) – characterized by the awareness that customers determine value and a willingness to change. Dominant question is "when?" Sensitive to changes in the marketplace that will erode its value.

5. The Pre-emptive Enterprise (mature adult) – characterized by entrepreneurial agility and focus on strategic clients. Dominant question is "where?" Always looking for emerging customer priorities where they will be able to deliver value and be highly profitable.

As executives lead their companies through these stages, they must realize the questions are cumulative. To truly get to the next level, the organization must have clear answers to the questions in the previous levels. Massive companies are able to buy time because they are not monolithic. They typically have multiple companies running within the larger company and operating at different stages of growth. Often, these smaller business units generate the cash flow and profitability necessary to finance the rest of the company.

In the end, I think we will end up with small nimble companies and massive companies. Mid-sized companies, who tend to be more monolithic, will be most at risk.

I think mid-sized companies have to avoid the pitfalls of large companies before, not after, they become large. Companies grow rapidly through systematization. Systematization reduces risk by forcing compliance. What leaders need to realize is they are enforcing compliance to methods that were known to work yesterday.

As there is no guarantee that such performance will continue to bring value to customers, leaders need to ensure that the most creative and innovative thinkers in their company are not constrained by administration and policy. Appropriately staffed sub-groups and a percentage of the company's profits should be continually set aside for exploration, while the bulk of the organization concentrates on getting returns from past investments.

Google is a great example of a recent mid-sized company that continues to explore despite its size. It is really two companies in one – OldCo and NewCo.

This strategic and proactive balancing act between exploration and exploitation is the only hope for mid-sized companies in a new reality of constant change.

Adrian Davis / December 21, 2011 / 4:23 pm

COMMENTS FROM 2012

IBM management: Running company into the ground

IBM's problems have been long-standing, and certainly not a surprise to those in the industry. The biggest problem that IBM has is that there is little, if any, organic growth of the company. IBM has entered lines of business by buying successful startups, but it has exited just as many, if not more. You name the IT technology--PCs, storage devices, networking, printers, semiconductors. IBM has either downsized those divisions, or sold them off to other companies. There are hot and heavy rumors as to which line of business will be next-- strategic outsourcing, or perhaps the hardware business (STG).

As you can imagine, this does not make for an optimal business environment, much less one that is pleasant for the employees. The resource actions, LEAN, cost-cutting atmosphere, etc. are all symptoms of the bigger problem, in that IBM cannot maintain high value for the business. To put it bluntly, management has run the company into the ground.

For their part, the top executives have focused on financial engineering — preserving stock value while they themselves cash out at opportune moments. IBM's 2015 plan is just another example in a long line of financial tricks. The real "crime" in this whole scenario is that people are confused about what IBM actually is. At its heart, IBM has become a financial engineering operation masquerading as a technology firm. The corporate emphasis is not on product or services ("content" per Steve Jobs), but on EARNINGS PER SHARE. Once you understand and accept that fact, everything starts to make sense.

You don't have to like it, but that's the way it is.

Former IBM Employee / April 18, 2012/ 9:10 am

Relocate or lose your job

This is a great series, Cringe, from an ex-IBMer who was RA'd last year after 16 years.

What you didn't mention was the other rotten aspect of the Dubuque, IA location – how they use it to save money on severance. The game is this:

- Send a letter/email to an employee who works in a remote location (typically a home office) telling them that in a few weeks their office is now in Dubuque (or Denver or wherever), perhaps with a token amount of money to help with relocation costs;

- Employee tries to discuss with their manager that the move to Dubuque is a hardship and they cannot make the move;

- The manager informs the employee that if they do not make the move then it is the equivalent of them quitting their job, hence no severance;

- Employee has to make a choice – move (mostly at their expense) with no long-term job guarantee or quit (with no severance).

If only IBM could harness the energy of the Watson's spinning in their graves over what a bad place their company has become...

Ghost of IBM Past / April 18, 2012 / 4:56 pm

Execs don't think IBM needs rescuing

You may care about IBM, I certainly do (I work there).

You might also think that all this activity will somehow 'save' the company. I can assure you that very little will change because the suits don't think it need rescuing.

So we will continue to do more with less, be frustrated by our inability to create the sort of quality products we 'really' want to create, be amused as the execs fluster about when a customer threatens to throw us out, watch the suits get their bonuses while we wait for our seven shares to vest in 2015 (it may be a carrot but it's a bloody small one) assuming we have not all be RA'd by then anyway.

We will continue to play the IBM version of Survivor called "the PBC Challenge" (losers get voted off the island) which makes you do stuff for the brownie points it garners towards your annual assessment rather than for any real benefit to the customer.

As far as can tell, it isn't actually any better in all the places the work keeps going to either. Sure they may replace one US worked with 5 Indians or Chinese or Martians for all I care but they don't have the 30 plus years of experience I have to fall back on and they are not getting any training either in the old stuff or the new stuff. How do you off shore, off-shored work? Where does it go?

The thing is, the people at the top of IBM are selling to the people at the top of big business and governments. They are selling a vision, an idea. Who cares if it does not work as well as expected. As song as it saves money, the target audience still come out ahead, their EPS goes up as well, their execs are happy. Sure, some like Disney see the light and walk but there's enough people out there buying onto the vision for them to keep going. Who's to say the competition is really any better at this level anyway?

In the end MONEY talks. IBM execs will only pay attention when the stock price and EPS drops through the floor, when the economy picks up and their sales and profits don't. Fact is though, IBM can still sell a good story and that's all it takes sometimes to keep going.

Me? I'll be there until I find another job or I get RA'd at which point I will be gone. I shall not look back, I shall not miss it, I shall not shed a tear (but it does look good on the resume!)

NobodyImportant / April 18, 2012 / 6:53 pm

IBM knew it couldn't deliver services

I recently left IBM (on my terms) after 11 years there. I was a key client interface on two different outsourcing contracts. I saw first hand how IBM management repeatedly told the customers they would see no drop in service by moving work offshore or to a GDF. IBM management was well aware they did not have the skills and experience that were needed to deliver the services. In some cases, even though IBM India was saying they did not have resources available, US management still insisted on the moves, so that budget targets were met. They had ZERO concern for the impact it would have to the customer. When customer problems arose, the mid to upper level management simply use the account team as the excuse and throw them under the bus. I saw how some jobs were hurriedly moved to Dubuque to meet employment targets with the local governments. Six months later, those same jobs were moved offshore to even less experienced people. I saw first hand how problem solving, by offshore resources, took exponentially longer. Even then, solutions usually had to be driven by a US based IBMer. In my educated opinion, these articles are very accurate and display the current management focus and culture within IBM.

Recently-departed / April 19, 2012 / 4:12 am

Execs have 'no clue' how to deliver

Love your breakdown about Dubuque, but it's not a new story. Look at the legacy IBM towns, Endicott, Poughkeepsie, etc. They were always strategically located away from cities to control the environment, to keep employees tied to them, making it difficult to switch to a new employer.

Gerstner turned IBM into a bean counting company, and the concept of creating value got tossed out the window along with 100,000s of dedicated employees. The executives and the sales teams have always made commitments to clients without a clue as to how they would deliver on the promise. IBM was a great company because they took care of their people, and the people somehow delivered on promises to customers.

Now that IBM no longer takes care of its employees, there isn't anyone left with the skills or commitment to deliver on IBM's promises (IBM has never had a culture of accountability, just annual reorganizations to shift responsibility).

Most people buy IBM because it's a safe decision, i.e. everyone used to say "no one ever got fired for choosing IBM". As corporate decision making shifts to younger people who grew up in a different world, the IBM buy decisions won't be automatic--and IBM will win less business because of their poor fulfillment track record, i.e. loss of Texas, Disney, etc.

tinagleisner / April 19, 2012 / 5:01 am

Maybe IBM represents all companies

So perhaps IBM is just a microcosm illustrative of the American business (not just IT) world at large.

Not to defend top IBM management, but as a thought experiment, can we put ourselves in their shoes? Their only real job is to increase shareholder value. What's the quickest and easiest way to do that? U.S. and Western European employees are expensive liabilities. Laws and regulations just get in the way. So why not embrace labor from developing countries? Why not make your company into a meta-contractor, so when something goes wrong you've got enough contractual complexity to shield you (or at least grossly delay) any kind of prosecution (see BP oil spill, or mega-banks in general)?

Yes, you *could* do the noble things, and innovate, focus on customer service and all that good stuff. But that's *hard*. What does the risk-reward curve look like for innovation and customer service, versus that of outsourcing and contractual complexity?

Responding to groups interested in IBM's behavior:

- Customers.
  I'll admit to being cynical, but these days, I just assume bad customer service is the way of the world. In my experience, big companies and lousy customer service go hand in hand. Good customer service is a boutique item, and comes at a boutique price.

- Investors.
  Warren Buffet is a pretty good investor, and he thinks IBM is on the right track. Besides, if IBM is changing its business model to be more like the big banks, I think they probably will be good to investors. The idea isn't so much to deliver actual products and services, but be a conduit for business to take place. A sort of "meta-broker" of technology deals: just make sure as much money as possible flows through your hands, skimming a little bit for yourself here and there.

- Government.
  In the U.S.A at least, the government is supposed to be representative of the people. I don't think the government acted in the interest of the people before, during, or after the recent financial crisis. With IBM, yes, the government *should* care, but like with the banks, they don't care (and/or are too incompetent to know better, and/or are corrupted).

- Parents.
  At least we can say, with IBM, we have an example of a company that does NOT eschew ethical values and behavior.

I'm not so much bothered by IBM in particular, as I am by all companies acting similarly to IBM. IBM is another drop in the bucket, as far as I'm concerned. "Our society is based on rules — rules that can't be ignored by CEOs of big companies." And who wrote those rules? And who enforces those rules? If we go back to the big banks, then the bankers themselves wrote the rules, and no one enforced them anyway. That's a pretty sweet position to be in, if you ask me. Even if you didn't write the rules, and someone is actually enforcing the rules, you can still evade them with a team of slick, highly paid lawyers working for and guiding you.

"You may be a cynic and say this doesn't matter, but look at your bank balance one day and see it's been looted and you'll suddenly care a lot, because that's where this is headed as the quality of our IT systems degrade." I know it matters, but short of voting and spreading the word, what can I do about it, besides being depressed?

When the day comes that my bank balance is looted, I'm sure IBM will be the least affected. They will have far too many layers of subcontractors, lawyers and liability release agreements in place to indemnify themselves.

Maybe if enough people get their bank accounts looted, there will be a class action lawsuit. And everyone affected will get some insult of a settlement, like $15 or a 30% off coupon for select IBM merchandise.

Matt / April 19, 2012 / 11:22 am

Customer systems info has no shareholder value

I've worked in IBM Services for years and the real sad part is that if you passed this list of customer system questions/requirements to a Sales Rep or an Account lead, they would struggle with the meaning of many of the terms. To actually gather the information would require a small act of Congress, not to mention a multiple-group fire drill. Eventually a report could be produced but it surely wouldn't be in one day and it most likely wouldn't be accurate. And all of this is because IBM management wouldn't view this as an exercise, which provides shareholder value. End of story.

Doomed-IBMer April 20, 2012 at 4:12 am

Realistically, the Cringely request to evaluate customer systems requirements would take several days, if not weeks, to answer. If they were not already part of the Service Level Agreement (SLA), then there would be a lot of negotiation between IBM's project or account execs and the customer.

While most people would rationally expect this sort of thing to be part of a managed IT service, the provision of these kinds of reports ON DEMAND is something IBM would not be ready to handle unless it were explicitly written into the Service Level Agreement. If such reports are part of the SLA, that's great.

In all likelihood, this would be considered a "special project", requiring explicit funding and a dedicated project manager. It would require the coordination of people from many different departments, some US-based and some offshore. All of these people operate within their own time zones, so instant timing is probably not possible.

You cry "this is a critical situation...the customer is demanding this info!" So what? Your typical system or network administrator inside IBM may handle 5, 10 or more different customers at the same time. If you want someone to set aside some time to put together the reports, then that's great...who's going to PAY for it? Let's set up some more meetings to discuss that part.

"Provide this info or we'll cancel the contract!" It's regrettable that the customer wants to cancel the IBM relationship. Just be sure to pay those millions of dollars IMMEDIATELY, per the contract terms labeled "premature exit clause".

Former IBM Employee / April 20, 2012 / 5:06 am

Performance review a 'farce'

A few of you mentioned PBC [Personal Business Commitments scale] ratings. I would like to comment further on this farce. Every year, the employee is required to fill out a portion of the PBC with their achievements for the year. At first glance, this sounds like a good thing. It's the employee's chance to prove their worth to the company and show management how they've added value to the company. However, the employee is never told that their PBC ratings have already been decided a month or two earlier.

The information the employee added to the PBC is totally worthless and management doesn't even care about anything in there.

Furthermore, Your PBC has less to do with job performance than it does with saving the company money. You are graded on a bell shaped curve. The management teams get together and rate everyone to fit inside that curve. The rating system is totally unfair, and is demeaning to each and every employee. It is not merit based, as IBM wants the employees to believe.

This year, top management came out with a new bell-shaped curve graph. They were told that 60% of the employee population needed to fit into the category of 2s and lower. (Also lowering the numbers of 1s, and 2+s that could be given out). Last year's model allowed 60% to be rated at 2+ and above.

At IBM, this is called raising the bar. It allows IBM to withhold a bigger chunk of the variable pay award (which is already far lower than other related companies in the industry). And it also allows them to forego giving the employee a raise for the year. It is another cost cutting exercise. But the employee thinks they don't contribute enough to the company. They increase their hours and work hoping to get a better rating the following year. It's a win-win situation for IBM no matter how you look at it.

Also, I want to add one more thing. The variable pay. Each year, each dept. is given a 'bucket' of money to hand out to each employee.

Did any of you know, that the executives ask for a kickback from that bucket of money? For lack of a better word, they ask for 'donations' from each individual pool to fuel more executive pay. This is totally voluntary on the part of each manager, but how many managers are going to bite the hand that feeds them. They end up giving up a portion of that pay back to the fat cats at the top of the food chain and the employee that was stiffed out of his raise for the year, is now also cheated out of some of that variable pay.

disgusted IBMer in the northeast / April 20, 2012 / 5:48 am

Auditors miss the point

Bob, you are exactly right. Even though IBM does use Applications and System Controls Accountability (ASCA), it is sketchy across the board. The auditors focus on meaningless data half of the time and miss the point of being "accountable". I just moved into a new department and the list(s) of diagrams, servers, and apps is sketchy at best. However, fixing IBM? That would require open-minded executives and there are none. I believe the problem with the way this company is run is the same as it was 30 years ago: The business does not understand IT--how it works and functions as a whole. The decisions made never have the best interests of IT, yet IBM is an IT company, which is kind of an irony, is it not? The tools and software solutions are available, the coordination is not there. Duh, I guess that would be bad management if they do not trust the IT department to do what it does best and that is the technical side. IT departments should be run by IT Engineers, Architects and Specialists, not HR or finance managers. Give us a budget, a model for expenses and we can sort out our own priorities.

Jobs-R-Going / April 20, 2012 / 6:00 am

Are customers billed accurately?

I think some of you are missing the point of this. Companies pay IBM millions a year to support their stuff. The costs are often based on the number of servers and applications. If IBM cannot instantly produce an accurate list - how do customers know they are being billed accurately?

Let's say a critical application that runs your business fails. Someone calls in and reports application xyz is broken. Can IBM instantly tell you what systems it runs on? Does IBM know this application is critical to your business? Lets assume IBM has a clue about your critical application. Do they know what software behind the scenes makes it work? Could they trace the data network needed for it to work?

The answer to most of these questions is usually "no". How long is it going to take IBM to figure out what is wrong, find the right talent to work on it, debug and fix it? Remember, this application is critical to your business. The longer it takes, the more money YOU lose. You've hired IBM to support your systems. Can they? How well?

John / April 20, 2012 / 1:49 pm

IBM leadership has 'failed'

Your articles are good to see and as someone who has been with IBM for some time I think you've done an overall good job capturing lots of points. It is, however, fairly service-oriented. You haven't really addressed what is going on in Software Group or STG, which is where products get made.

From my vantage point IBM management does not understand what it sells. It does not understand how to create much less sustained efforts to create and market products. IBM servers and software are not any better than it's competitors. IBM *COULD* be the Apple of the business world, but it's not. For some, the perception from the glory years remain and they think IBM is more than worth it but the reality today is buying IBM isn't a good choice.

These things are fixable. The change, however, is a management one. I doubt there is the motivation. Failure of product/services just results in more layoffs.

There was a time in the not so distance past where inter-site rivalries were quite bitter. Gerstner put a stop to that. As a result, it didn't matter where one was located, we focused on what was right for the customer, what was right for making product.

The management-enforced "rivalry" now is inter-country. Preference is being given to India and China, who both have very poor track records when it comes to IBM accomplishments. Brazil is much better. But it doesn't matter what makes good engineering sense. It doesn't matter what is right for the customer. India, China and Brazil are the answer over and over again. The skills aren't there, as Bob has rightly observed.

IBM needs to change from a system fixated on minimizing engineering costs to maximizing the sale of top quality systems, software and solutions for revenue and profit. IBM needs to be blind as to location and cost of employee and get back to quality. Apple does this and they are fabulously successful. There's no reason why IBM couldn't and shouldn't be as well.

It's funny, but U.S. employees, for instance, have currently four-year cycles to get an update to their current office workstation or laptop. It doesn't matter if the laptop can't do the job. Nothing will be done until the time period is over. It's not uncommon to hear about employees going out and buying their own replacement just to get their job done.

IBM employees are dedicated. It's IBM leadership that has failed.

I would like to hope your articles would turn things around at some level. I do know some executives within the company get it.

StillAnIBMer / April 20, 2012 / 1:51 pm

IBM will 'fail': How bad will it be?

This low cost, low skill, no experience global resourcing strategy is not limited to the services part of IBM. It is hitting product development, maintenance and support with the result of products that are so bad they cannot be sold or have to be rewritten by experienced people in the U.S., the UK, Canada, Japan, Germany and other highly developed nations. It is also hitting virtually all IBM processes that effect customers from sales, to ordering, to fulfillment, to billing, to service. Literally everything that effects IBM internally and IBM clients/customers is being off-shored as fast as possible to cut costs.

I see the effects and the failures of this daily. Customers are leaving, others are upset and suing or threatening to do so. These resources cannot do the job, yet IBM rewards them by giving these incompetents more work to do. The executives literally do not give a damn – all that matters are the short-term numbers, making that 2015 target and collecting their bonuses.

We have our own name for the "2015 Roadmap" – we call it "Death March 2015". The company will pick us off one by one until there is no U.S. personnel left other than the boots on the ground required to service machines. The hall talk is that these survivors will become contractors – perhaps sold off to some service company like Qualserv. The experienced craftsmen and women who used to design, build and support product have been pruned out of the business through getting RA'd solely because of maniacal cost cutting.

If IBM had to write a new operating system from scratch, there is no way the company could do so – the skills and experience are gone. IBM can't develop its own new software either – the software portfolio innovation is through acquisition of agile, innovative companies that build products IBM wants. Then IBM croaks off half the employees of the companies they buy, effectively killing off the innovation machine they just bought.

IBM executives are such morons – they actually expect US employees to implement "Death March 2015" and to sacrifice their own jobs for the good of the company. This after IBM declared war on its U.S. employees when they misused Lean to dump employees. Every quarter, you live in fear that you will be sacked. To be sitting between an executive and his bonus is a terrible place to be.

Services executives continue to deny there are problems, meanwhile blaming U.S. employees for the failures of their overseas counterparts. But the bean counters are happy whenever the penalties for missing SLOs are less than the savings of using global resources. Net – the money counts, quality and adverse impact on the customer doesn't.

IBM services clients would be well advised to hire some IBM services business castoffs that know where and how IBM works (or more aptly said doesn't work). We know where the dead bodies are. Last, as an IBM vet with 30+ years of service, I can say that IBM is now one of the worst companies to work for in the US and is doomed to fail. The heart and soul of the company is mortally wounded – it is too late to change course to recover.

The question is not whether IBM will fail, it's a matter of when and how precipitous the failure will be.

Frank / April 20, 2012 / 9:36 pm

ROBERT X. CRINGELY

IBM is just 'average' now

The premise that IBM can be fixed is faulty. The company can't be fixed. The IBM that many of us knew and loved 20 or 30 years ago had some key qualities – excellent customer service and respect for the individual (employee). If you take care of your customers and employees, your investors will probably do well too. When I joined in 1992 to do operating systems work, it was a long dream come true.

Old IBM had problems – it was bloated with many people who essentially retired on the job. Performance problems were not dealt with using the existing mechanisms because people were too afraid to hold others accountable except in the most egregious cases. Groupthink dominated. Old IBM was not sustainable and there had to be changes to make IBM a little leaner, a little more agile, and a little less risk-averse.

Lean doesn't have to be mean, though. In the last 10 years, the culture has devolved from "respect for the individual" to "office survivor." For 364 days a year people are supposed to team and collaborate selflessly – and then on day 365 somebody gets thrown or voted off the island. The unrelenting drive to cut costs instead of growing revenue has had some nasty effects on employee morale and the quality of products and services. In the quest to become competitive, IBM has become average. And you can't charge above-average prices for average or below-average products and services.

Pockets of resistance exist in IBM, but they are aging out. You can't turn time backwards; you have to move forward. The new IBM isn't the core problem – it is a manifestation of problems we have as a society. IBM was able to grow and prosper because it had the benefits of our society; a good educational system, clean air, a reasonable government, etc. IBM now (and many other companies) doesn't seem to recognize or care; they owe no allegiance to anybody. (See "mercenary" in the dictionary.)

I'm proud to have worked on some great projects with some great people while I was there. But I'm dismayed to see what happened.

Mike April 21, 2012 at 2:24 am

Global Services: 'Smoke and mirrors'

I took a buyout at the end of 1997, with 30 years at IBM to protect my retirement plan & medical. At the time I worked for a Sr. Director who worked for the CIO who worked for Gerstner. A year later I came back to IBM in the same job as a contractor/consultant. I was working

146

for a manager, who worked for a Director, who worked for a VP, who worked for a SVP who worked for the CIO who worked for another SVP who eventually reported to the CIO.

In less than a year, Palmisano had destroyed the "flattened" management and added all these layers of managers, who contributed nothing, because none of them wanted to "own" anything. It was all about not being responsible for delivering anything.

As part of the Global CIO team, I had the opportunity to sit in Randy McDonald's (Head of IBM HR) office and listen to him spout off about how he only wanted people at IBM for an average of 5 years, and how people were just replaceable resources. It's this style of management that has contributed to the most talented people leaving IBM, either through RAs or resignations.

I now work for a Business Partner, and see the attrition that is damaging IBM. We find a good IBM salesman, who will work to close deals and deliver value to the customer, but IBM either forces that person out (to "manage income") or they leave for a company that will actually pay them for what it's worth. IBM is no longer the pre-eminent sales company that it was through the 1980's. Global Services has always been a smoke & mirrors organization, with the true cost/value of contract hidden in a maze of complex deals.

The "Gerstner Turnaround" was really all about re-branding "Mainframes" which had gone out of "style" as "Servers" and then selling more of them at less profit. Everything else was in cooked books and smoke & mirrors services deals.

OldSgt / April 23, 2012 / 6:59 am

IBM becoming a software company

Although I'm a former IBMer now (by choice, not by decree) my colleagues and I frequently said that the internal actions by the company only made sense if one looked at it through the lens of a divestiture.

Not only does that make sense in the abstract, it makes sense in the here-and-now. IBM hardware is a commodity, as are most of the services that clients and customers want to buy. The truly "value-added" services needed to make Smarter Planet solutions actually work are interesting but not in great demand.

Plan 2015 is about doubling earnings, not revenue. Because it is mainly labor, services will never have the gross margins of software, which can be up to 70% or more. Software doesn't call in sick, can be downloaded , and can be sold again and again.

Therefore, software is increasingly where IBM is placing its chips (so to speak). IBM is becoming a software company; nothing less, and not much more.

Njia / April 24, 2012 / 6:03 pm

Services: A low-margin product?

· I think this is right. We buy a lot of software at high costs and then are bound to long-term contracts at blinding rates for ongoing licensing and support. That's a pretty sweet model if you can manage to establish a product just right. The development costs to IBM are negligible, and once a large company settles on zSeries or DB2 or WebSphere or even Notes it takes a lot to justify the effort and money and disruption a change would take. If you view IBM as a financial holding operation, then services is a low-margin product being rapidly marginalized by low-cost international competitors while enterprise software has a very high cost for competitors to enter the market and a serious lock-in inertia for customers.

Cris E April 25, 2012 at 9:27 am

IBM could become like Oracle

To say that IBM deliberately cheated its customers oversimplifies what's really going on. While cheating was certainly part of the game, there was also a LOT of wishful thinking on all sides. Both customers and IBM executives believed in things like "self-healing infrastructure", "on-demand computing" and the like. Both IBM and its customers made massive investments in technology and services they did not fully understand. Sometimes the investments were profitable, and sometimes they were not. Let's just say that the lack of understanding on both sides came at a huge cost.

If IBM becomes like Oracle, then it's going to become a MUCH smaller company — and not just because of the loss of services. IBM hardware is no longer all that unique. They have mainframes and large-scale storage, but in the distributed server space they're just one of many players.

In software there is a similar story. IBM has some compelling products, but so do many other companies — not to mention the fine open-source and "free" offerings that are available in the world.

Lousy margins aside, one of IBM's major value propositions over the years was that it offered an all-inclusive package--hardware, software and the services needed to tie everything together. IBM sold a lot of hardware and software over the years using services as a loss leader. Without services, what's IBM's value proposition over Oracle, Microsoft, HP and everyone else? Why pay IBM the big bucks?

I'm not disagreeing with your proposition, by the way. IBM could very well become like Oracle. But in a world where both hardware and software are rapidly commoditized, what kind of player will IBM be?

Former IBM Employee / April 25, 2012 / 11:50 am

IBM will become just a 'marketing name'

Gerstner merely delayed the inevitable at IBM. He beat out C. Michael Armstrong (career IBMer) for the CEO job because Armstrong advocated breaking up Big Blue.

Armstrong, true to his vision, went to be CEO of both Hughes Aircraft and AT&T and broke them up (liberated shareholder equity) and sold off the pieces. CEOs who can build a business up are rare nowadays.

IBM will be a marketing name for some Chinese manufacturer in a decade or so.

Sammie Saheee April 25, 2012 at 1:54 pm

Lack of details in contracts causes chaos

Time for a brief reality check: When I was with IBM, I saw strategic outsourcing deals from multiple angles. I've seen deals being negotiated by the sales and customer executives, and I've seen deals in place that actually had to be serviced. I participated on both sides of the fence. As has been reported by many observers, there were (and probably still are) multiple disconnects between the sales side of the house and service delivery. Deals (service agreements) were written with a LOT of wiggle room. They had to be — if deals were written with the detail expected by your typical IT specialist, programmer, what have you, then the deal would never get done. The details would be too many to mention in a contract.

In some deals, there would be line items like "Manage 50 UNIX servers" or "Maintain backups for 25 Windows servers", with absolutely no accompanying detail. No back-up schedules, no retention requirements, no up- or downtime specifications, etc. The idea was that those details could be filled in later on, but often they never were. As you can imagine, this often became a recipe for chaos.

IBM's problems in outsourcing come from a fundamental conflict among three things: What was agreed to in the contract, what is actually expected by the customer, and what can be reasonably AND PROFITABLY delivered by IBM.

Sometimes, this conflict could be resolved. Often, it could not. The bottom line is that a lot of deals were signed that didn't bring in enough money. In such cases, IBM executives made decisions on what they could do within the bounds of each contract. For some deals, IBM would take a loss and deliver to customer expectations. For other deals, IBM would wiggle out of it somehow, often paying significant performance penalties. It's no secret that corners were often cut so that the deal could be serviced.

It is nice to think that "IBM should live up to its social promises and do the right thing, no matter what". Such expectations are not realistic. At the end of the day, IBM made a lot of the hard economic decisions that their customers were either unable or unwilling to make for themselves. That's what you get when you outsource your operations.

Former IBM Employee / April 26, 2012 / 7:35 pm

'The process is the cancer'

I might tend to agree with the three problem areas you mention if it wasn't for the fact that every new account wasn't a complete mess. If IBM cared about their customers or their reputation they'd do something to resolve these issues.

Reality check: The reality is even if IBM were able to write a good contract with clear expectations they still couldn't deliver because as Cringely already pointed out "The process is the cancer" and IBM's answer to every problem is to create a new process.

Example:

1. Takes six tickets for one change. Three native customer tickets per change, than three native IBM tickets to track

the three customer change tickets. Multiply this six- ticket process by five groups included in the change and you now have 30 tickets opened and closed for one simple change or install.

2. Takes anywhere form two weeks to two months to get ID's created that are needed to log on and manage an account. Usually you'll spend half day just trying to find the process needed to get ID's and another half day trying to find the right groups to do the work for you. This will all vary for each account and changes constantly so it may take longer.

IBM's Global Delivery model is completely broken and won't be fixed because no one above the 1st or 2nd line manager wants to hear it. If by chance someone does point out the model is broken and doesn't work the response is, you're not following the process so they add some new process to help ensure the old broken one is being followed correctly.

iBummer / April 26, 2012 / 10:19 pm

'Huge drop' in productivity

I agree that IBM's delivery models are often broken. I'll respond to your examples with a bit of half-a**ed explanation as to why things are the way they are.

When IBM's outsourcing business started, there were two huge problem areas that management needed to urgently address: Accounting and accountability. As the outsourcing deals progressed, there was lots of activity. Much of this activity was covered by the service agreement, and a lot of it wasn't. It was the part that wasn't that concerned IBM's management—for although the activities made sense in terms of servicing the customer, it was something that wasn't part of the contract and IBM wasn't being paid to do. Sometimes, this "unauthorized" activity wasn't even authorized by the customer's own executives.

In a typical self-managed IT shop, "creating user IDs" and "making changes" are often handled as business-as-usual activity, with minor change control and tracking if there is any at all. If you need something done, you find the right people, contact them and they do it. If there is a problem, you work things out among yourselves and "do what it takes to get the job done".

As part of an outsourced deal, this was considered unacceptable. Every activity that took place within the deal had to be approved by someone (for accountability) and tracked (for proper accounting). So over the years, IBM consultants, project managers and executives created vast systems of change control processes and procedures. The goals of accounting and accountability were indeed met – but there was a huge drop in productivity. Activities that were once routinely handled in an instant were now huge productions, requiring approvals and notifications of God know how many people before completion.

As operations spread across multiple delivery centers, the drops in productivity became even more pronounced. Activities that were once handled within a single delivery center (e.g. RTP or Boulder) were now handled across multiple delivery centers, each with their own responsibilities. As operations spread to offshore sites, there were additional issues. Communications and cultural differences became problematic sometimes. Language was an obvious barrier, but so were vacation schedules and off-days. If you're in the U.S. needing something done quickly, it's no good to be told that your counterparts in France and Germany aren't around because they have a mandatory vacation day or national holiday.

At the time I left in 2010, IBM management had been working to eliminate personal contact between groups. For a lot of stuff like creating server IDs or managing network devices, you had to submit requests on an internal website. Each request would go to an anonymous person somewhere in the world, who would do the work and respond to you when the work was finished. Communication was via the website, or by anonymous e-mail using a common address. I remember playing detective sometimes, trying to figure out who was responding to my own service requests. That way, I could contact them directly by e-mail or telephone when issues arose. You can imagine how this level of "personalized" service impacts productivity.

Former IBM Employee / April 27, 2012 / 12:27 am

Complex process for simple tasks

That describes exactly the reason for upcoming paths my agency is taking. The ability to get the work done is stripped from us by removal of access, removal of tools, compartmentalization of tasks to the exclusion of cross-training, and layering ever-increasingly complex processes over the top of the simplest of tasks.

I've been in IT for nearly 40 years (and in one agency or another for 36), I can't take it any more. SLA that can't be met BECAUSE of the processes heaped on after those SLAs were negotiated, no mobility because of the compartmentalization, morale that's in the dumpster throughout the agency.

I don't want to quit. I love the work. I can't stand what it's turned into. I'm out.

Fed Up Fed / April 27, 2012 / 7:58 am

Process means no progress

Sounds just like the Fed agency I work for. Everything is process, process, process, all to generate a bunch of management reports that have almost nothing to do with what is actually happening in the real world. "Get the job done and keep the user happy" has become "Follow the process, hit the completely arbitrary SLA's and who cares if the work gets done or the user is happy". It's hard to believe even a "suit" could think this is progress, but somehow they do.

Another Fed Up Fed / May 1, 2012 / 8:25 am

Outsourcing ourselves

Cringely, you got it right a few columns ago. IBM is a "sales" company.

They sell to the press, to the government, and to their employees, in addition to their customers. They used to be interested in solving their customers' problems. The only customer problem they're interested in solving now is: How much money does the customer have, and how do they get the most of it for the cheapest cost to them?

I was at a conference for the highest-performing technical folk in the company a few years ago. In the exec Q&A, techies were asking for advice in how to stay current in technology – a requirement – given no time or access to tools or education. And in answer, Nick Donofrio – the "godfather of the technical community", who reported directly to Sam Palmisano – said (I quote): "Your jobs are going to wherever they are cheapest on the planet. Get over it."

About the same time, at an IBM Academy of Technology meeting – which only the so-called technical elite of IBM attends – Nick told the attendees that IBM had just hired 15k people in India. Problem is, they couldn't identify the technical leaders among them. What he wanted the attendees (us) to do, is to identify the technical leaders among those Indians, and mentor them. I.e., to outsource ourselves.

These are the same execs that keep talking about how the U.S. needs more highly skilled workers. These are also the same execs that lay off a number of employees who asked for a few unpaid months off, to finish technical PhD's that they have been paying for out of their own pockets. If the execs are telling the top techies in the company this, what do you think their attitude is to the rest? This has been a strategy that's been playing out for years. The path has not changed, and neither has the hypocrisy.

On another topic: In 1999, IBM froze the pension plan. Now they're pushing the last of the employees on those old plans out. I remember reading some provision in the law whereby once the number of people covered by a pension plan drops below some bar (number? percentage?) a company can "cancel" their pension plan completely, and remove it from their balance sheet. With the newly announced "transition to" plan talking about it allowing improved business planning, I'm wondering if 2014 is the year we'll see that happen? – a plan that's taken 15 years to play out.

And then, the only employees left will be truly variable costs. Other than the executives, of course. The only way their costs vary is upwards.

gone / May 5, 2012 / 9:40 am

IBM's 'sociopathic' ways

A company that operates in an entirely sociopathic fashion is almost always cooking the books somewhere. If 100% of your corporate objective is to pump the stock price (with 0% in creating a skilled and loyal workforce) you will OF COURSE find a penny or two here and there if you need it to make your quarter.

Sometime in the next five years, IBM will have a earnings miss, and that will be followed by certain inquiries into accounting practices, followed by restatement of earnings for prior periods. Put it in the bank.

Khadijah / May 6, 2012 / 5:48 am

Competent tech workers must be a priority

I used to work on a lot of outsourcing jobs for IBM, particularly in server and storage management. Although the "billable hours" mindset and foreign labor issues are important, the more immediate issue is having a competent staff in the first place.

Although IBM has a lot of warm bodies, the simple fact of the matter is that IBM does not have enough competent staff to deliver on all its outsourcing contracts. When I left the company a few years ago, there were just a handful of people (I was one) that were capable of implementing, configuring and troubleshooting a SAN [Storage Area Network] . Most people within the company at the time had no idea what a SAN was, and probably still wouldn't know today.

Server and database management is in a similar position. To adequately monitor a database, you need to know what parts of the database to monitor, how to set it all up, and an action plan when the monitoring detects a problem. IBM has the tools, but it does not have the depth within its outsourcing staff to adequately implement and use them. The needed skills in database and systems management are simply not there in sufficient quantity.

In most companies, this level of competency is ingrained in its employees using formal training classes, plus supplemental learning in test labs as well as on-the-job training.

At the time I left the company, the only training that IBM was offering to the outsourcing staff was basic project management courses. The test labs were being disbanded, with equipment (servers, workstations, etc.) either being sent to India or sold on the open market. Some items like SAN switches and storage devices never really existed in quantity — the management didn't want to spend the money.

To add insult to injury, IBM's outsourced employees no longer had access to IBM's software collection. Software products like AIX, DB2, Tivoli and Websphere were once easily downloadable by employees for internal use. At the time I left, this access was disabled. To get this software, you had to requisition the software via official requisition channels, and provide a funding source. That's right — IBM outsourced employees had to BUY the software just like any customer.

So when I hear about customers dumping IBM for stuff like not monitoring the servers or performing the backups properly, I'm utterly saddened but not a bit surprised. This outcome was baked into the cake long ago. Although it's tempting to blame the problems on H1Bs or laying-off workers or whatever, the customers are leaving for a much simpler reason. All too often, IBM is proving itself to be incompetent to perform the work for which it has signed up.

Former IBM Employee / June 15, 2012 / 1:34 am

They have the tools, but they lack the talent.

Still the stock market keeps rewarding IBM for their financial performance. The question you need to ask is when will all this catches up with them in the market? Only then will executives have incentive to re-engineer the company.

Stephen Johnson / June 15, 2012 / 5:23 am

COMMENTS FROM 2013

Promises not delivered

IBM headed downhill in 1995 when what we had been promised in writing every year of my career simply vanished. I resigned and walked away in disgust after Gerstner and the board decided they deserved our pensions more than we did. (Pocketing pensions to drive the stock price up so they got bonuses was what cash pensions were all about.)

Even before that IBM clearly wanted to eliminate CEs (later called SSRs). They thought they could have us simply dump our knowledge into a database and then anyone could fix anything.

When they claimed they were going to get customers to change out their own parts (in live mainframes) I knew they really had no clue at all. Even we did not feel comfortable pulling 440V power supplies out of running machines and they thought they could get customers to do it? That's nuts. Truly insane. They seem to forget that the reason they sell equipment is because "IBM Means Service". Silly us – we actually believed that. Get rid of service, and the next contract is not automatically yours.

We routinely broke contracts sold knowing full well there was no way we could meet the terms. We went into accounts requiring secret clearances because there was only one person who actually had one and he had to sleep sometime.

When I left it was primarily because they had downsized us from 18 to 3 and my phone rang almost every single night. I was so exhausted I was falling asleep driving. First my manager avoided me for a week, and then he offered me MORE WORK for the same pay to stay. Hysterical. And clueless. They never replaced me.

Gail Gardner / March 25, 2013 / 5:13 pm

IBM makes it tough for employees to be loyal

This post is very accurate. Especially this quotation: "[Policy changes] are handed down from on-high by a management generally out of touch with reality, yet simultaneously determined to share as little information as possible with employees." It's this approach that is a HUGE problem and it's destroying U.S. morale. I understand that business changes are inevitable; you have to grow revenue and continuously balance the books, but why can't you be at least partially transparent about what you're doing and why? Be up front that you're cutting the U.S. workforce to drive a larger business strategy. Be honest that you don't even know how to solve the problem of growing revenue and you're going to try a lot of different approaches and hope one sticks.

At the same time, IBM seems to have this ridiculous expectation that employees should be loyal. They are fairly disgruntled when critical talent (like myself) leaves for a better opportunity. Oh, sorry, were you being loyal to me when you, without any notice, walked a team of contractors out the door without transitioning their projects, so now the regular employees are picking up the pieces because you didn't think you needed a plan? Were you being loyal to me when you cut the 401K-match program and vehemently denied layoffs are coming? Were you being loyal to me when you assured me that you're not sending U.S. jobs to Asia and Africa, but did it again and again and again?

There is also a lot of mindset that "this is how it is everywhere. This is the best company in the world to work for so just suck it up." Yeah, that's why I found a great job with a company that is focused on investing in its U.S. workforce to grow U.S. revenue.

RecentlyFormerIBMer / April 23, 2013 / 2:43 am

IBMers in 'survival mode'

IBM used to talk about its people being its greatest asset. Then the yearly employee survey disappeared. Then everything down to pencil erasers needed business justification and three levels of approval before final SVP approval. Then, the "thank you" gift program where peers can send small gifts to others for their achievements only had napkins with the IBM logo on them (sarcastic but not too far from the truth), which ultimately became an eHallmark card type of recognition program. Then the internal IT help desk disappeared and what remains is that after a few days tickets automatically close because "multiple attempts to contact you were attempted with no response".

Then, during yearly reviews you are reminded you are getting a low rating because of what happened two years ago by a set of first line managers who are told what to say by their second line and HR. And if you pushed back on your manager, they had the ability to rewrite the review to make some "clarifications". One would think all of the above is a little stretching; alas it is FACTUAL.

With all of the great things that IBM had at its disposal, it has created generations of IBMers that for the most part are in survival mode now. While there are many individual managers who excel and truly care about customers, shareholders and employees, they are dwarfed by the majority of folks who talk-the-talk and do not walk-the-walk. IBM leadership as a whole continues to fail in small ways every year and maybe, just maybe, the cracks are beginning to show.

Note to Ginni: To what end is simply achieving the EPS numbers when clients and employees are treated the way they are? IT is a complex business, no doubt. However, when a company as old as IBM cannot make it in the top 100 of all respected companies in the world, and IBM claims to be a global company, all that experience and chatter just seems to be superficial and stems from arrogance; and others are beginning to take notice.

Trembler Wallace / April 23, 2013 / 5:08 pm

'Smoke and Mirrors'

Bob, you wrote, "IBM executives are fixated on the 2015 plan." You got that right.

"At some point IBM will realize its 2015 plan has already failed (remember you read it here first). IBM's stock price will drop a lot."

Don't underestimate the ability of IBM to use financial tricks to make the 2015 plan. The 2015 plan is all about reaching $20 EPS (earnings per share). As earnings disappoint and share price falls, IBM just buys back stock. Less shares = higher EPS even as earnings fall. Fewer shares also keep the dollar value of the stock high even as the market cap of the company falls.

Ginni isn't making money on the market cap of IBM. She's making money by cashing out stock options and Restricted Stock Units (i.e. a gift of stock that an exec needs to hold for a period of time before they can sell it) . Over $50M worth in the 18 months since she became CEO. And the execs at IBM keep collecting more of these gifts every year, then they turn around and use the company's money to buy back even more stock, inflate the price of the stock and make sure that they can cash out the gift for big bucks.

You may be right. IBM may be a sinking ship but don't count out the execs' ability to keep her afloat and even hit the 2015 EPS goal. It may require throwing a lot of people overboard to lighten the load but they still have a lot of smoke and mirrors in the financial toolbox.

BlueFluLou / June 21, 2013 / 10:52 am

The 'best and brightest" aren't staying

Sigh, so IBM misses its 1st quarter revenue numbers. Ginni blames the sales force, the dwindling, less mature, largely 'acquired' sales force. Revenue has been flat for a LONG time, primarily because the sales force is in constant churn (large dollar sales take a long time, and usually require a decent relationship with the customer, which the constant sales churn prevents).

Amazingly, despite the sales territory churn, and reduced "feet on the street", the revenue has actually remained flat, not declined. My opinion (34-year IBMer in software sales) is that the constant decline in, or churn of, the sales force has finally caught up with them and at this point revenue will likely not recover. This latest layoff has actually reduced the number of sales personnel, and there is no way that the remaining folks can provide the sales increases that IBM needs to turn this trend around. At this point, the 'heritage IBM' people (the older ones like me, with the historical IBM view of the job where pursuit of excellence was the main thrust of customer support) are mostly gone, and the remaining sales teams have gigantic quotas, and even if they make it are more likely to have management cap their earnings than reward them for it. Look at the trend, faster processors and servers, requiring fewer software licenses to accomplish the same work, gigantic quotas with little chance of getting adequately rewarded even if you DO make the number, and only an expectation that next years number will be 25% larger than the one you didn't make this year, and you can see that the "best and brightest" are no longer staying with IBM. The ones that I know that have left in the past couple of years invariably made more money with less stress. IBM is in much more serious trouble than the market understands.

TomB / June 21, 2013 / 7:26 pm

Those cast off won't become IBM customers

There is also another force to be reckoned with. There are thousands upon thousands of laid-off/ex-IBMers all over the world that have a bad taste in their mouth towards the company. Every time one of those ex-employees lands in another role that involves IT decisions (i.e. purchasing hardware, software, support, etc.) you can bet that "old-bitter-taste" will rear its ugly head. They know how IBM operates, what they had to deal with and alas, how they were cast-out off like yesterday's wet newspapers. Do you think they will sign a deal to bring IBM's products and services into their new company? Heck no. As the number of ex-IBM employees grows, so does the number of ex-IBMers landing in roles in other companies. All this adds up to less work for IBM. They're killing themselves and they are too haughty to realize it.

Just another number / June 21, 2013 / 9:45 am

Holds off purchase till after 2015

Exactly. I left last year and now advise on HW purchases. Firm was looking at a new mainframe mid-2013; I suggested we hold off until after 2015. Want to guess why? Smile…

me, too / June 22, 2013 / 1:09 am

Cut executives from the ranks: No one will miss them

I have worked at four other software companies, two of which are effectively out of business. Both of which followed the same model IBM has been employing for the past several years:

1. Not recognizing that the least expensive sale that can be made is the second (and third) license of a product to a very happy customer,

2. Not realizing where the real revenue is coming from – maintenance and upgrades, and not investing in current highly profitable product line to keep that revenue stream healthy.

3. Thinking that the front line technical staff is interchangeable parts.

4. The belief that "we can acquire our way out of stagnation."

This model is often seen in companies where the executives have been away too long from the trenches, so they don't accept responsibility for complete delivery of a product. Where failure is glossed over at the top levels, and brutally punished in the ranks.

IBM can return to a position of preeminence in the technical world. It will require sacrifice on the past of the leadership, not the workforce. It will require a new vision rather than a continuation of failed and failing policy. Quite possibly the best thing that could happen right now is if half of the executives were fired on July 1. It would be months before anyone noticed they were gone.

GottaLoveIt / June 22, 2013 / 6:22 am

Yes, the "Smarter Planet Club" won't be missed

GottaLoveIt said: " Quite possibly the best thing that could happen right now is if half of the executives were fired on July 1. It would be months before anyone noticed they were gone."

LOL! Here is a current example of IBM Bloated Management's "Smarter Planet Club".

Take the VP of something called Global Smarter and Innovation Alliance Solutions.

This VP has only 4 people reporting to him.

An isolated case you say. But his boss has the title General Manager, and this GM has only seven other people reporting to him (mostly people with the title of "Director", but who don't have anyone reporting to them, so what is it that they are directing?). The entire chain of report for this GM is 12 people. That looks more like a 1st line manager's role than a General Managers role to me.

But wait, there's more. That GM reports to another GM, who reports to a Senior VP, who reports to the CEO. So you have Director>VP>GM>GM>Sr.VP>CEO Lots of Managers but no one producing anything.

If all of those managers were fired July 1 as GottaLoveIt suggests, who would notice, indeed. That's your Smarter Planet at work.

Aruba Johnson / June 23, 2013 / 9:18 am

Serve revenge "cold"

I got dinged five years ago and, as they say, revenge is a dish best served cold. In my current IT job, IBM software will NEVER be recommended as it's worse than garbage, only fit for the thieves (oops, high prices consultants) in Global Services; I use OPEN SOURCE stuff which costs little or nothing. Let the IBM Software Group go bankrupt with their crappy, expensive acquisitions. I'll only "consider" their lousy crap when Hell freezes over.

me 3 / June 23, 2013 / 3:28 pm

Managers laid off employees and took their jobs

At my university, in business law classes, I studied briefs on IBM and how they rewarded risk. Well I was a relative (four-year) newbie with the company when Gertsner took over. A lot of the old time IBMers who retired and have medical just can't swallow this, but it's all true. I saw a good company go south.

In the mid-1990s, I watched managers lay off employees to save themselves (i.e. they took their job). I was under the old pension plan and got caught up in the layoffs in 2007. I warned a friend it was going to happen to him, too, and he called me a nut case. A few months down the road, sure enough, he was gone too. They have been getting rid of the defined pension people for years and they don't do it in one big swoop so as to not attract scrutiny. Now, I didn't have to train my replacement because I'm sure that she/he just took on extra workload. I went from a team of three to me. It was horrid working 6 a.m. - 10 p.m. everyday and most weekends (because I was worldwide). If I didn't make my numbers I got dinged, whereas if the execs were failing they just moved to another division without any accountability. It's too bad. It used to be a great company. I went to school part-time to get my degree so I could go to work for IBM. I'm sure Watson is rolling over in his grave...

Vicki / June 23, 2013 / 2:19 pm

Customer: Had to work with angry ex-IBMers

A few years ago, IBM signed a new and big deal to provide services for a company. I was assigned to work on that project. At that company were scores of ex-IBMers. IBM eventually lost the deal mostly through its own screw-ups. However those scores of ex-IBMers were in the front of the line in bringing attention to each and every one of IBM's problems. When they could, they helped contribute to those problems too. While 95% of the problems were IBM's doing, we were definitely operating in dangerous territory and the ex-IBM team was ready and motivated to ambush us at every turn.

IBM has seeded the corporations all over the U.S. and the world with enemies. I run into these people on almost every assignment. When your treat a very large workforce poorly for over a decade, it will come back to haunt you. Beware IBM, there is now a very large army of people working for your customers and against you.

VERY TRUE / June 24, 2013 / 2:57 pm

The "inner circle" -- then everyone else

As an ex-IBMer (I left a month ago – not part of the RA), the IBM equation has worked for me. I got fat stock options and retention packages in both cases and left again after they expired. I have watched the incompetent and inbred management team blunder through the same three-four-year cycles. Most of those in senior management have been there for 15+ years and are well protected from above and below. Above are more managers and below are a slew of disposable employees.

I have seen IBM under Gerstner, and then Palmisano/Rometty. You can tell how the old guard has taken over the reigns again and has enjoyed the trajectory the more cerebral Gerstner put them on. Palmisano was a master schemer. His background was all about that having come up through the hardware division.

Rometty is but the last step of his scheming – just see the RSU he scored compared to the ones she's on and who set the boat on an unsustainable course and jumped off when it was clear there would be more icebergs than open water ahead.

The employee base is under skilled, under motivated and underpaid because of chronic underinvestment. All the internal (dis)enablement is so weak and underfunded that it is a mere veneer of appearance. If you judge the sales force by the training targeting a 10-year-old veteran profile, if is easy to see how either management's understanding of field sales is limited or the average skill level of the force is woefully inadequate.

The software group (highest profit margin area) is under huge amounts of pressure. You can see this by how they stuff so much unneeded product in their substitution lists in all the large Enterprise License Agreements. You can see this by the way their salespeople are pressured (beaten) into submission and for the first time in my career I have seen a sales force solely driven by a spreadsheet. The sales force is woefully underpaid but seem to be happy when they are offered symbolic pay rises with more strings attached that a fly in a spider's web.

You see, IBM is an enterprise infrastructure vendor (despite their fantasy of wanting to cater more for the mid-market). In the software world, this requires a special breed of sales skill and mindset. Not transactional (like order takers selling Microsoft) but much more knowledgeable expert sales people. Especially in the Tivoli and analytics area. IBM has managed to break this down and "sellers" are now pressured to just show their $200K per month. There is no long-term pipeline, domain expertise has been destroyed (they just love to see sellers as door openers) and there is endemic top-down mistrust of the organization.

IBM's huge cost savings could be achieved by changing their internal IT – they are doggedly hanging onto two dinosaurs of IT: Lotus Notes and Siebel (the latter just being replaced by a Sugar CRM derivation). This drives up the cost of sale hugely. Notes is hugely inefficient and their CRM mess requires them to have different tools for reporting, forecasting, planning and customer views. All this work is pushed down to the salesperson as opposed to back-office (they got rid of those in the early 2000s) and doing cadences with line managers, interested parties and anyone who needs direct first hand data are the norm, so much so that one could reliably speculate 40-50% of a seller's time is spent in internal management.

Nobody cares. Too many insignificant, yet protected and well paid jobs go to the ones who can correlate data from multiple data sources and create a single view in Excel for some manager who needs it to justify why they exist.

It is a misery to see such a great brand, which in the past century managed to survive all the alleged reporting of mixing in with less desirable aspects of the 20th Century history (Nazi Germany, Apartheid South Africa etc.), fall to its knees because of being failed by inbred management.

Gerstner broke the mold, shook up the business based on good business principles (he was not a technologist) and set it on a solid trajectory only the blundering backstabbing old guard took 2 decades to break down.

I think IBM needs to ensure management always has some 50% of fresh blood to ensure it changes with time. It needs to shake up the management team and move out the 30+ year veterans who still have fat pension plans and are protected from any mistake. Nepotism is so visible especially when you have family relations of senior managers enter the workforce and out pace their peers.

It is a culture that clearly shows the existence of an inner circle and "everyone else" and it is failing the one party they, themselves market as being at the forefront of all strategy – the shareholder.

Free / June 26, 2013 / 9:47 am

Spot-on remarks

What an insightful and totally accurate assessment. Speaking as someone who has been on the inside of IBM for almost 20 years I can confirm to other readers that your remarks are absolutely spot on.

goinggoing / June 26, 2013 / 1:08 pm

Customers will catch on, and bail

Since Gerstner left, IBM has resorted to the old habits of bloated layers of management, non-responsive management, and plain old poor or nonexistent management. I swear this is true. I had a 2nd line manager who promoted one of his managers to a project manager and then started calling himself a 3rd line, hoping to be promoted to a director, and of course he was. I used to have four managers between Gerstner, and me now, I have no idea who I even report to after my 3rd line. I think there are eight layers now, I have no idea what any of them do except run status meetings and travel back and forth from the U.S. to China, Singapore, and Mexico. I have had the same manager for almost four years and I have never met them in person. Yet, they rate me, they rank me, they decide if I am a good employee or not. It is a joke. The company is being run by accountants and it shows. The customers will soon see this and start bailing even faster than they are now.

Almost gone / June 26, 2013 / 5:45 pm

VP says bullies now run company

I am an IBM Exec – a middle ranking one. Unfortunately your column is correct in most respects. IBM's Armonk management has lost the plot. The company is now run by clueless, out of touch bullies. It hurts to say it but its true.

VP / June 28, 2013 / 2:26 am

More execs; fewer do-ers

The VP response is accurate, as is all the IBM commentary by Robert. I am equally close to decisions in software. Too many chiefs covering themselves and ensuring their career growth, vs. driving the business. The latter only matters in quarterly results, not business decisions.

IBM hires more execs and lets go more of the doers. That is the M.O., and it will continue. India has huge developer turnover so output is down, as is quality.

I had hope Ginni would be different than the train wreck Palmisano. However if there was any indication of that this was a false hope. IBM only knows how to sell concepts, not build and deploy solutions.

And it has no idea what they are doing with cloud. Case in point, Oracle just made their dreams of being cloud relevant irrelevant. Kudos to the samurai CEO for covering his own poor cloud strategy with those deals. Executives have no clue about software and have shown this. Dump your stock, leave the deck chairs and get into the life rafts.

another on inside / June 28, 2013 / 11:18 am

SmartCloud and PureSystems "a disappointment"

IBM is investing but hasn't been successful. On the organic side, IBM has one of the biggest patent portfolios. But the IP hasn't translated into top line growth. Recent major organic efforts have been very disappointing: SmartCloud and PureSystems. Amazon winning at CIA? Even internal assessments said EC2 was superior to SmartCloud in terms of capabilities and price. At a product line management and technical leadership summit in Raleigh, one manager called Pure his biggest flop. On the inorganic side, most acquired business failed to live up to unrealistic expectation. First, business plans must have "synergy revenue" to justify the premium required to outbid other suitors. Cognos once grew over 100% and it was still not good enough. Second, acquired capabilities often die a death of IBM complex process, financial controls and legal paranoia. A company- wide task force had to be formed to save the SaaS roadmap 2015.

IBM Cloud Hahaha July 25, 2013 at 3:14 pm

Palmisano "rebuilt" the bureaucracy

Gerstner was brought in to cut the fat and he did. Management as well as lots of dead wood was cut and rightfully so. Without Gerstner it was likely that IBM would have been in the pickle they are in now, only 20 years ago. But, Palmisano comes in and rebuilt the bureaucratic empire all over again filling positions with cronies and "yes" men. Gerstner had management chains down to about five, maybe six, levels.

We are now back up to 11 or more levels of management. No surprise IBM is where it is today.

BarneyFyfe / July 1, 2013 / 12:35 pm

IBM is hiring "C students"

Couple of points:

1. China got hit in the last layoff as well, they really didn't discriminate. They made such massive cuts that a number of hardware projects are now left in a state where they do not have enough people or the right people to try and make a go of it across the world. A lot of people feel this is the beginning of the end for the M in IBM. If you read the shareholder statement you will see cloud computing up 700% but that is only because they bought the innovation. IBM has cut so much out of R&D that now they pitch ideas, wait for others to figure them out, then buy the companies outright. Innovation that matters?

2. Interesting how ignorant the upper management is when it comes to this stuff. The CEO is out giving talks about the need for companies to hire more people than needed to help stay ahead of technology when her own company has less than needed to support the future challenges. Not to mention her own company is in the news each year for layoffs.

3. The employees at IBM don't know who is in charge anymore, the answer is more than likely HR, which thinks that it has saved IBM. They hire a diverse work force, but in doing so they bend the requirements for the diversity numbers. The reality is while others are hiring the best and brightest IBM is hiring the C students to become more diverse. With all the exceptions let in the people around just do not have the drive or the understanding to be able to deliver on the new challenges.

What does it all matter? Really IBM has enough money in the bank and through revenues to be able to be less of a hardware company and more of an investment company. The current model is to buy what is profitable and use that instead of innovating. They think that contractors are the best routes, not always because of cost savings but because there is no press when they cut them (often, and you would be surprised how many high level don't know this, the contractors cost more than just keeping the employees around).

Will the M in IBM exist in five years? More than likely not. But I think the company will be around until you see something like a wide-scale depression. With only services to offer, and greatly marked up services at that, with no real product line to fall back on they will be very suspect to any wide scale market downturn.

Norman / July 19, 2013 / 1:42 pm

Nothing substantial available in IBM's pipeline

Regarding the patent portfolio: An IBM CEO once joked — "good ideas do not come out of IBM research, they escape." We can't blame the gifted people who work in IBM research. The problem is sales people manage IBM. They simply do not understand or would appreciate a new idea for a product or service. They see things only in terms of what they can sell.

Guess what? IBM is selling less every quarter. There is nothing in the product pipeline that would stir up a lot of new business. When you have nothing substantial in your product pipeline then you have to retain your existing customers and business. IBM isn't doing this.

Customers are an excellent source of information and ideas for new products and services. Guess what? IBM is not listening to them. IBM's increasingly bad service is dominating their conversation with the customer.

It is sad. IBM is truly managing by the numbers. Number of patents. Earnings per share. Increasing profit from existing businesses. Make those numbers better. Ignore the other numbers that warn you of future problems.

John July 26, 2013 at 10:54 am

Current mode of operation is not sustainable

Once one gets their head around the fact that IBM has decided to become Wall Street's bitch rather than actually making new things that businesses want to buy, everything makes sense. As long as the EPS hits the target, Wall Street doesn't care what happens long term. That's the fundamental problem. No one cares about the long term any more nor do they care about how the results are achieved. The stock market is full of folks who want to be rich this quarter, not 10 years from now. Those in the know will ditch their stock and walk away with millions. The only time people will care is when it all finally blows up (Enron, mortgage/banking melt down are good examples). The current mode of operation is simply not sustainable over the long term.

Mike July 25, 2013 at 7:06 pm

Under current management, IBM's customers are biggest losers

A large number of the people in the U.S.A. doing support and managing projects are contractors. In many parts of the world, IBM's customers get okay service from its global centers (India, etc.). In the U.S.A., the service is not so good because it is in the middle of the night in India. The best people don't work that shift. This cost cutting action will shift more work off shore, and sadly it won't be done as well.

I want to be clear and fair here. There are many great people working in India. The U.S.A. perception of their support is really a factor of time zones. Let's be honest — if I were working the graveyard shift my work probably wouldn't be as good. If IBM served its U.S.A. customers from Argentina, Brazil, Canada, or even Ireland the time zones would be closer, people would be more awake and more alert.

As IBM squeezes its budgets and people, the work has to go somewhere. It goes to the cheaper labor and things suffer. In the end the customer is the biggest loser. They don't get a price break when IBM swaps bodies on their account and projects.

John / July 26, 2013 / 6:29 am

Can't wait for crash

Bob, as usual, you are spot on! Can't wait for the crash to happen soon enough... can you say 1-3-9 and illustrate that please on a PowerPoint slideshow to fawning comments from India and elsewhere??

New_Blue_Mantra / July 27, 2013 / 5:05 am

IBM "toxic"

This is how dead-serious lay-offs are so that 'numbers' are made. Certain areas of the business need more employees. Some of the RA'd people have those skills. Upper human resource personnel in GBS WOULD NOT REMOVE THEIR NAMES FROM THE LIST. They had to be laid off and then, if they wanted to, reapply externally. This how toxic IBM has become.

The decision wasn't even coming from those high level HR execs in GBS (I could name names but I won't) it was coming from above them – in Armonk.

So, many important decisions are made by a VERY few people in IBM, and no one underneath that precious few stands up and says "no".

McGee / July 27, 2013 / 5:21 am

What is 1-3-9?

1-3-9 is basically a bunch of slogans and stories.

The slogans are "All IBMers have:"

- ONE Purpose – To delight the customer

- THREE Values – Dedication to every client's success; Innovation that matters; Trust and personal responsibility in all relationships.

- NINE Practices – Put the client first; envision future; share expertise; restlessly reinvent; dare to create new ideas; treasure wild ducks; think-prepare-rehearse; unite to get it done now; show personal interest.

Then to inspire IBM'ers, there's a bunch of apparently submitted stories that demonstrate the above values. Most of these stories are reminiscent of melodramas you find in Reader's Digest or TV shows. They all begin like: "John Smith was a 37-year old IBM'er having coffee on a rainy Monday morning when he got a phone call..." or "For the last twenty years, Mary Jacobs has believed in one thing – there was a solution to (some) problem".

Then the stories go on to tell tales about how there was this time when an IBM team saved lives in a hurricane, how a client was in deep shit and IBM team saved the day, how the U.S. Postal Service still lives because of IBM, how IBM is helping the DEA wage war against drugs, how IBM teams are making a difference from rain forests in Borneo to primitive cultures in Africa. etc.

Vampires may have taken control of IBM but Bram Stoker or Anne Rice is definitely not chronicling their tales.

Montana / July 27, 2013 / 11:10 pm

A slow implode

A whole team of worker bees was let go in the U.S effective 7/31 -- their jobs moved to Costa Rica. The ENTIRE management chain was left intact. NOT ONE manager was laid off. It's been said many times that the company is top heavy with management and executives. So, we have managers left in their jobs that manage 2-3 people. The company is doing a slow implode.

Where is Ginni? She's like Waldo.

Anon / August 1, 2013 / 1:50 pm

Can you say "Titanic"?

Yep, pretty much all of GBS management survived the last round of cuts, even those who were moved around (can you say "playing musical chairs on the deck of the sinking Titanic"?) no longer have ANY direct reports. What are they doing? Nothing other than "talking business" and running to meetings, collecting big paychecks, but there are few new business deals. And Ginni fiddles on!

Top Heavy / August 1, 2013 / 6:34 pm

A 'lack of cohesion' in IT industry

I was recruited into Andersen Consulting about 20 years ago as an experienced hire as a systems analyst and designer for building manufacturing systems. The day I walked into the place a strange ripple ran up my spine. I soon learned how they, and other big consulting firms worked:

1. A high profile, power type senior partner sells the project

2. Once the contract is signed, the partner gets on a plane to sell to another company, meanwhile a school bus pulls up and a lot of young, bright, attractive, but inexperienced kids pile off.

3. For the first half of the project nothing gets done because nobody knows anything, though they act like they know everything, and so they fight to determine who are going to be the chiefs and who is going to be the Indians.

4. A last minute scramble takes place on the last half, to last third of the project, to get something of a 'deliverable'

completed.

5. Their real "core competencies" were to somehow make the failed project turn out to be unavoidable, yet still no one's fault. Client management often buys into this because they are on the hook for making the crappy decision to hire the consultants.

The industry suffers from a lack of cohesion, which might have produced acceptable standards, like the construction industry appears to have – but perhaps part of the reason has to do with the rapid pace of change in technology. But every decade new has a new set of terms and spins on methodologies. But I don't think that they've actually changed in substance. You still have to do requirements gathering, model your existing environment, then model the future target environment, then design in detail around that target, then develop, test and roll out.

Another thing: Good project managers are like good salesman – it's an innate skill that has to do with knowing how to manage people, especially technical people. But too often it's seen as a vertical rank, and so you get ambitious people who not only don't know how to manage people, but quite often hate people, to say nothing about trying to provide some constructive usefulness to clients and the economy overall. Sadly, this is what has happened to IBM as an organization.

TimK / August 7, 2013 / 10:44 pm

Short-term profits over productivity

And the cause for the problems at both IBM and Andersen Consulting were exactly the same – focus on short-term profits at the expense of building a productive business.

IBM wants to make the bankers on Wall Street happy with their 2015 profit goals, and to hell with the business.

The partners at (Accenture / Andersen / the Big 4 / name your own consulting firm) want to pick up the largest amount of cash at the partner payout party, and forget the idea of actually cooperating with the customer to build something productive and useful.

In both cases, simple things like good project management are sacrificed to increase the profits of a few guys who wear white shoes.

Ryan / August 8, 2013 / 7:59 am

'Poor' corporate culture

Folks like Amazon, Google, Yahoo, and others quickly grew their business and systems well past the traditional computing model. They had to develop a new infrastructure and application design. To these firms, the "cloud" is a highly capable service that is super reliable and inexpensive to operate. IBM is still stuck in the traditional computing model and doesn't understand the full nature of cloud computing. This becomes obvious when you look at their cloud offerings.

Folks like Amazon, Google, and others became wildly successful because they were open to new ideas and were willing to challenge the validity of traditional forms of computing. IBM has a stunningly poor corporate culture — new ideas are rejected, communication is guarded, management doesn't listen.

John / August 8, 2013 / 7:22 am

IBM culture: A 'quasi-caste system'

Great comment John, especially the last sentence. I spent over two decades at Big Blue and witnessed the corporate culture take a rather steep nose dive, particularly as the senior leadership became infiltrated with 1970s and 1980s business school MBA graduate types brain-washed in "shareholder value" theory. They were not, nor never have been, technical in nature and therefore were unable to grasp the wide-scale technical requirements of a large project, such as in the examples you mention. It simply wasn't in their one-dimensional capability.

Worse, the condescending way they viewed and interacted with the technical 'help' was beyond indignant. The culture began to resemble a quasi caste system for lack of a better analogy. The execs were the landlords, the techs the low-level serfs. If a tech sent an email to an exec, nary a response would, or should, be expected.

The most glaring example I witnessed was when a senior project manager once said to me, "The success of a project must be viewed as 5% technical and 95% customer perception." I quickly reminded this non-technical PM that if the technical aspects of the solution do not function properly, no amount of perception would make up for a failed computing implementation. But this PM was adamant about his stated premise. I knew then, more than ever, how leadership viewed these projects and being a long-time (and rather talented, I might add) IT technician, this flew in the face of what I had witnessed and learned over the course of 40 years pressing the keys. My gut feeling was 'these people do not have a clue.'

I knew then, particularly with the ramping up of offshoring and endless layoffs of talent in the name of EPS, It would only get worse going forward. Therefore, I left and found an opportunity where they appreciate solid technical talent. From what I hear from former co-workers, the talented are jumping the Big Blue sinking ship in droves, especially as the economy has improved. Even more so, as companies are drifting back to the in-sourced model, opportunities for those who can are sprouting every day.

Never before has it been truer – buyer beware!

Joe / August 8, 2013 / 8:56 am

Vital signs weakening, IBM 'in distress'

There is the old saying, "the operation was a success but the patient died." Shareholder value, EPS, are not the only measures of a successful business. There are many other measures and their needs to be a balance in what is expected. If you focus too much on a couple of measures, you will miss other important data points and make poor decisions. IBM is so fixated on the 2015 plan and the quarter-to-quarter earnings statement, it is failing to notice its vital signs are weakening, organs are shutting down, and the company is in distress.

John / August 8, 2013 / 11:37 am

IBM 'just lets things break'

Many years ago IBM decided it was more profitable to do a less thorough job, run the risk of failure, and pay the penalties for those failures. They figured they were spending more on quality than they would if they just let things break. This decision, this mindset has spread through the whole company. If you can get by not doing something, don't do it.

Since then customer satisfaction has suffered, business retention is poor, every contact is challenging. IBM is so desperate for new business they will do anything to get it, then do their best to lose it.

Philip Crosby made the point in his book Quality is Free. When you have imperfect quality you spend a lot to fix it, deal with it, manage it. You should see how many people IBM has today "managing" the mountains of problems on its accounts. You should see how many hours their DPE's and SDM's work and the stress they're under. IBM is now paying dearly for their poor quality. IBM's quality problems have now become a cancer to the organization and its long-term viability. This is not something they can continue to "manage through." Until you fix the source of the problem, the massive problems will continue.

Another John / August 8, 2013 / 7:50 am

IBM stands 'idly by' while damaging customers' business

Good point. IBM's internal governance is equally bad. The quality of the "global" support is poor and out of control. Backups could stop, security patching could stop, and no one will speak up. Even the most basic work has to be checked and documented to ensure it is being done. Very few things just work automatically inside IBM these days. Everything has to be managed and tracked.

...

What AT&T is doing to IBM and IBM's customers is unbelievable. Any other company in the world would have called AT&T on the carpet and read them the riot act years ago. There is probably no oversight by IBM. IBM seems to be unwilling to acknowledge things are not working well and something has to be done. IBM certainly will not, or cannot take any action. If a partner were damaging your business would you stand idly by? IBM would.

Ginny / August 8, 2013 / 12:16 pm

Execs just don't 'get it'

The problem with IBM project managers is that none of them is technical. They are all prided and rewarded on being PMP, senior PMP, senior specialized executive certified PMP or whatever it is they like to add to their email signatures. What do project managers who have no technical knowledge and don't understand what the implications of a technical project is do? Well, they manage scope and change. Any evaluation of a technical requirement, which almost always results in something else for the better, especially in the software world, is considered scope change by these morons and for which you have to go through some ridiculous change management process to implement, and to which they object because they just don't get it.

bob / August 8, 2013 / 5:22 pm

Beatles' songs spoof IBM

I'm just disappointed that I spent nearly three decades honing my denial of what the people at the helm were really about. I bought into the "corporate values" and the rest of the rah rah (e.g. "six sigma quality", "transformation"), all the while bucking inner suspicions that nothing of lasting quality could come of the endless stream of clueless personnel and technical decisions, or of career promotion being proportional to obedience, while inversely proportional to hard work and innovating first in one's approach and methods, and then in the products themselves. My 3 rating in January was a stunning display of what I want to call business mental illness.

Please enjoy some Beatles songs spoofs[2] inspired by too many hours of scratching my head over the ongoing insanity that I experienced while attempting to develop software in that psychotic environment. Some of the lyrics were inside jokes for coworkers at the time, but many will ring true to anyone who had what they imagined to be a career there. The music[3] and lyrics[4] can be found on that same website.

That said, I thought their separation package was generous. But even so, I kind of miss my identity being heavily defined by my deluded sense of working for the best company, a company that I believed respected individuals, and was with me in being committed to every client's success....

Steve, August 8, 2013 at 6:30 pm

IBM 'messes with clients'

Regarding the post from Bob that is a very good observation. Thanks. If you look at most construction, highway, or manufacturing projects you will find the PM has many years experience in the field and has some technical skills. If IBM were to bid on a bridge project they would not get past the first round on bidding. Quite bluntly, the sales person and the project manager would be unable to answer the questions asked. Perhaps that is a key to the problem.

For years, IBM has been notorious for going to and selling to the execs of a company. They bypass the technical folks, middle managers, and schmooze their bosses. Senior managers in most companies are not

---

[2] http://jethrick.com/gdbeatles/

[3] http://jethrick.com/gdbeatles/tragical-rometty-tour.mp3

[4] http://jethrick.com/gdbeatles/tragical-rometty-tour.html

"technical." That is not a criticism, they have special talents for what they do, and it just does not involve designing computer applications. Yet IBM targets them and finds ways to keep "those in the know" out of the meetings.

Somehow, when IBM fails they are always forgiven. That is another of IBM's interesting talents. If I were selling parts to a factory, didn't deliver, and disrupted their production — it would be a very cold day in you-know-where before that factory would consider doing business with me. In most lines of work you never, ever mess up your customers business. But IBM is doing that every day — and getting away with it.

If people familiar with application development, or system management were involved in the decision-making process, IBM would get a lot less business. When IBM would make a sale the expectations would be clearly defined, the results would be monitored, and there would very little wiggle room. Like everyone else, IBM would be expected to deliver what it promised.

IBM's use of generalist project managers is yet another indication of how IBM views its business and its customers.

IBM does have some very good project managers. However, this too is a skill IBM believes it can ship offshore and do remotely. When you are building that bridge, there is no substitute to watching the crew pour the concrete. It is easy to see if the concrete supplier brought you good product. It is easy to see if the crew knows what they are doing. Doing things remotely over a phone using a second language is a very poor way to manage a project. But as we can conclude from these columns, IBM does not care. They're selling to our execs, not us.

reply to bob / August 9, 2013 / 11:48 am

Project managers' certifications have zero value

@Reply to bob, you are absolutely right – I was on a call a few weeks ago for a GBS project and the project manager had no idea what she was talking about to the customer. It was an embarrassment to hear someone who was talking about anything but technical facts. When the customer asked a few technical questions, she was struck dumb, and then deferred to the technical folks like myself on the team. Yes, IBM has some very good PMs, but the majority of these certified PMs are non-technical people who got an IBM certificate, stating they are IBM Certified PMs and IBM Certified Executive PMs and act as though they have the ability to walk on water and better.

These certificates have ZERO value in my opinion, if said PM does not know what he or she are talking about! I would never hire an IBM Certified PM without a rigorous grilling, because it would be a total waste of money to do otherwise.

Right on August 10, 2013 at 4:34 am

Tale of two projects

An Indian PM got a hold of an old internal timeline for discussion and planning purposes only. He then presented it to the customer as a deliverable commitment! He then turned around sending out notices for status meetings, demanding action plans leaving folks to go, WTF? No one had any idea that the project was approved let alone resources committed. The customer was displeased to say the least.

Another PM found a virtualized product schedule slipping so altered the Gantt chart to make it appear that things were OK and on schedule. Just before the delivery date someone noticed that there was no testing! Snapshots of the Gantt chart were found showing original dates and that a test section did exist earlier.

Minimal testing was squeezed in, and to the horror of the PM, one client could see and access the data of another.

PMHell / August 11, 2013 / 2:43 pm

Indian engineer: Too many low-skilled workers here

Regarding your comment on emerging markets, I am a high performer (1-rater as they call it in IBM) for the last 3 years in IBM India.

Some points that I have noticed over the last 8 years of my career at IBM India :

1) No smart engineer in India wants to work for IBM. It has a reputation of workplace with a lazy, flexible work environment that is often abused by employees.. WFH does not stand for Work from Home, though it is famously called "Work for Home" here.

We have such a hard time hiring anybody who can THINK. That is the reason why U.S. folks struggle to work with us.

2) No tea/coffee; No two-wheeler fuel reimbursement; broadband reimbursement amount keeps reducing every year. This year,

pay hikes have been pushed out by a quarter.

3) This company has a culture of hiring and retaining managers with very low or zero technical understanding of work. In fact, I know of cases of low skilled technical employees who were offered managerial positions.

To the best of my knowledge, IBM is the only place where this happens.

4) No company has transferred jobs to emerging markets without proper knowledge transfer at the pace at which IBM is doing it. I don't think other companies are stupid to have not thought of it.

5) Lastly, everybody here realizes that we cannot survive without the U.S. folks (I have only worked with U.S. folks so far, but these comments can be extended to other countries as well). We do not have the skill or understanding to make things work. This is related to the 1st point that I mentioned above.

It is matter of time when even we will be let go, simply because we cannot make great products without smart folks like you. The remaining average to high-skilled people here are already making their exit plans to escape the humiliation of inevitable lay-offs (including me).

My sincere regrets to people who have been RA'ed and hope that they find better jobs outside.

Emerging market IBMer / August 12, 2013 / 12:19 am

China consultant: Same thing here

I agree with your statement on emerging markets, just change India with China, and here you go. One thing different is that they are hiring language graduates (English, Japanese, etc.) then training them on the job because there just simply far too few computer science graduates who can speak a second language other than Mandarin. I can't even imagine how many U.S. and Indian (yes, they support us as well) supports got RA'ed in the end...

China IBM Contractor / August 17, 2013 / 7:26 am

India worker: Smart workforce seen as 'expense'

The entire India STG team feels hurt with the last RAs impacting U.S. workforce. I can assure you that there is no feeling of "getting more work" here, and in contrast people would like to show solidarity with their U.S. counterparts. There is no doubt that the U.S. team that heavily contributed to the growth of IBM brand so far is very essential for the survival of the company.

Cutting U.S. workforce is like shutting engines of an aircraft midair to save operating costs. It sure helps in the short term, but you are a gliding aircraft and it is only a matter of time before a disaster strikes you.

I hope IBM execs realize the gravity of the situation an act selflessly. You cannot run the company with new hires from emerging markets. If it were as easy why would not the exec and CEO positions be moved to emerging markets?

I can sense the morale of U.S. workforce dropping, and I can sense the engineers in the emerging markets also on the look for a job in a more sensible company.

It is funny that a tech company 2015 roadmap is EPS of $20. It seems we do everything it takes to get us there even if it means killing the smart workforce, which is being looked as an expense.

India IBMer / August 18, 2013 / 7:41 am

Another India worker: High performers penalized

Very well said, I fully agree with the above comments. The clueless STG managers are walking through the corridors chanting "ALL IS WELL" and showing a ppt that has a 5+ years product roadmap, while the smarter employees are making an exit. I wonder what would happen to the non-performers who grew so far by being loyal to managers. I do not even want to think about what would happen to the managers, who are technically challenged (not all, but most of them) and not fit for the outside industry.

It is this very set of people who encouraged a low performance work culture here in India. The low performers who were loyal to the managers were rewarded and the high performers who come with some attitude were penalized. They were cutting the branch in which they were relaxing. Now the fun begins.

STG IBM-India / August 18, 2013 / 8:39 am

IBM in 'death spiral'

Flashes of ENRON come to mind and I believe that the IBM Company will implode in less than five years from now; at ENRON (a big company), everyone thought the company would carry on indefinitely, regardless of what happened when the fraud was discovered. Well, we all know what happened there! You have a similar situation at IBM where executives and managers pump up the company stock price, work on huge buybacks and inflate the stock value to Wall Street; but internally the company is in a death spiral and nothing but the husk of its former self. In a panic, they rush out any buy any companies (not sure if the executives carry out due diligence here) that seem potential winners, as long as they can claim to the world that they have a full portfolio of products and services.

But ALL the past and present IBM executives in the world – Rometty, Mills, Rhodin, McDonald, Van Kralingen, Sanford, Horan, Clementi, Miller, Daniels, Moffat, Palmisano -- can't pull it out of the tail spin that the company is currently in. They wish they could but it's too little too late. The company certainly isn't going to celebrate its 200th birthday. Sad but true! I'm sure the Harvard Business Reviewers could write an "unbiased" book on the IBM story if they chose to, but that won't happen since IBM gives them big donations. I'm sure it would make for good reading 20 years from now.

Kudos to Cringely for keeping up the pressure on IBM management and keeping everyone in the know !

History Repeats Itself August 18, 2013 at 11:52 am

'Road kill 2015': Outsource the execs instead

IBM has many faults, not the least of which is the Roadmap (Road kill) 2015 where the IBM Management have well defined plans to take out 40,000+ US employees by hook or by crook before 2015. Why, as I type this, they have been furloughing STG employees and contractors until the last week in September 2013! You would have to be blind and deaf not to see or hear all these things happening inside IBM.

Administrative assistants to all executives except the biggest crooks (oops, I mean VPs and senior VPs) in the U.S. have been told that their jobs will be outsourced to remote administrative assistants in Malaysia by 2015. That's a lot of good U.S. employees whose jobs have been unnecessarily outsourced, because they have the misfortune to be working in the wrong place (IBM) at the wrong time. At the same time, no senior executive positions have been outsourced or cut – they are merely transferred to new positions around the world and get to keep their high executive salaries and then return back to Armonk after their "tour of duty".

Senior executive positions ought to be outsourced too, particularly those in bands 9, 10 and higher who make U.S. 150K or more every year. Think of the cost savings if you get rid of 10 of these executives – more than a million dollars in clear SAVINGS ! And consider that you will be cutting down a huge unproductive bureaucracy too; this is particularly noticeable in the CIO's office where you have so many layers of managers reporting to more managers that you have to wonder how they get any "real" work done. And these are senior people at band 9 and higher who rarely come face to face with ANY IBM customers! Something is wrong with this picture but it's unlikely to change anytime soon. And consider that you have productive support staff in Atlanta whose jobs have been transferred to support staff in India and China who is not only incoherent, but also not able to communicate clearly in writing. Is this the way that IBM serves the customer better? Or worse?

Think40 is another of those Ginni PR scams – just promises of education available to all IBM employees at the beginning of 2013, but guess what ? There is no money in any group's budget to take "real" classes ANYWHERE. Just ask any manager in SWG, GBS, GTS, STG, Research or elsewhere in IBM – truth or fiction?? Technical excellence?? You must be joking ! It is nothing but sell, sell, and sell even if it is ice to the reluctant Eskimos.

It is the IBM management's fault to give the U.S. stock market incorrect numbers and false expectations if the reality is different. That comes down to communicating the truth, even if it is unpalatable. If a bunch of cowards run a company on a pack of lies about how competent they are, then bad things happen when they do not deliver results as expected. I notice with interest that there is no mention of the Business Conduct Guidelines particularly where IBM executives and senior management are concerned. Yet there have been lots of mentions of violations by IBM executives and management all over the globe in the press; these days, the IBM name is more often associated with dishonesty and a disregard for the work undertaken and quality of the products sold to customers. But it wasn't always this way – at least it wasn't 25 years ago!

IBM successes are getting smaller and smaller. IBM no longer gets the lion's share of Federal project work but has to share projects with other vendors like Wipro, Accenture, and Tata etc. That is the reality of how the mighty have fallen.

A former great executive at IBM, Bob Moffat, once said "if you want loyalty, get a dog". I am not aware of any open internal blogs or wikis inside IBM, which tolerate any critics – they have been silenced if they are critical of any executive decisions. The Jams are a joke too! The results have been decided very much in advance by the IBM executives, on what agendas they would like to see advanced for their benefit.

So, please consider these observations and take the actions you deem appropriate.

Elephant In The Room / August 22, 2013 / 7:35 pm

Education is mandatory, but just doesn't happen

Think40 is not just for sales. It is for every employee and is mandatory. Education is key--except this year when travel was approved for annual education in Poughkeepsie for their premiere product line in 1Q, and then the ostriches said, "Oops! Not this year! No travel for you!" You will do the best you can with what you got. Yet execs travel and come and go as they please, all in the interest of keeping customers happy on the golf course and at the steak house. From what I have seen the travel is to put out fires, not so much to thank customers for their recent purchases. Oh that's right. WHAT PURCHASES? We have zero revenue but incredible profit year to year. Just how does that work anyway? And Wall Street is snowed too (with other phony stories from other phony profits with the Fortune 500 crowd). Ginni is desperately trying to turn around the morale, which is in the toilet. Jams, Think40, internal blogs, all of which no one has time for. Its as though she would love to see IBM as "fun" place to work (think Google). Well, it ain't fun anymore.

Barney Fyfe / August 26, 2013 / 7:31 pm

Think40 not good PR

Ginni Rometty announced Think40 earlier this year, and the video was accessible to every ibmer on the intranet. She said explicitly "no financial restriction". Six months later, first line managers still could not get written answers on the implications. When asked, HR and finance partners would never clarify whether employees could register for a conference (5 days X 8 hours = 40) under this program or not. They would only say Internet podcasts qualify. In practice, it further degraded management's credibility as it simply turned into a cheap accounting trick – record in a database when you decide to follow a free khan academy class. Think40 is one illustration of how PR works in this company.

Deadbeef / August 27, 2013 / 2:23 am

Training program is a 'joke'

Internal blogs and Jams. Ha ha. No one in their right mind says what they really think so you may as well just shoot any career you might have in the foot as do that. A few (very few) folks skirt around the issues from time to time, try to point out the flaws without being suicidal, but in general most people just keep their heads down. Discretion being the greater part of valor and all that.

As for Think 40. It started out as Ginni 'encouraging' everyone to improve his or her skills through various training opportunities. She even said no restrictions to location or cost, but then of course added it was subject to budget limits (and since no one has any budget for anything let alone training, we all know were that went). Then the 'optional/encouraged' Think40 training became a requirement with tracking, so now we are expected to all do our 40 hours and log it as well. Me? I do more that that every year just learning new stuff on my own. I have always done that, it's the only way to stay relevant (dare a I say "essential"?) in the technology field today. If you want stability, go drive a trash truck. It just galls me that this so-called training is little more than a joke with managers suggesting that if you attend tech calls, the sort of thing you just do 'as part of your job' to log that as your Think40 training time and call it done. Hardly in the spirit of the thing, is it? So I'll do my normal thing, I'll continue to learn new stuff in my own time and I'll log some of it just to keep the idiots in management happy and avoid another black mark on the ole PBC, but is it a real initiative?

As for the negative feelings, I suspect that most people are pissed simply by the total lack of respect (in spite of the so called "values") that the company's senior management shows to those who actually earn the money while they pay themselves bonuses. I'm not saying IBM is unique, but a little honesty would go a long way. Instead we get feigned concern and underhanded tactics used to keep everyone (including local governments) in the dark. I'm not denying that IBM has to change to survive but there are 'ways' to do that that do not alienate half the workforce and, in that respect, IBM has missed the boat. The point is that

IBM's customers are not blind either to what is going on. On the plus side, the competition is not a lot different either so what is a hapless customer to do!

nobodyimportant / August 27, 2013 / 4:50 am

ABOUT THE AUTHOR

Robert X. Cringely has been a Silicon Valley journalist and character for more than 30 years. An early employee of iconic companies including Apple and Adobe Systems, Cringely began his career as an engineer then transitioned into reporting and analysis, first at InfoWorld and since 1997 as one of the first Internet bloggers, first at pbs.org and now at cringely.com. His work has appeared in magazines and newspapers throughout the world including Forbes, The New York Times, Newsweek, MIT Technology Journal and many others. In addition to InfoWorld he has worked as a columnist for Inc. and Worth magazines and ASCII magazine in Japan. His previous book, Accidental Empires, was published in 18 languages. His television documentaries made primarily for PBS and UK Channel 4 have aired in more than 60 countries. Cringely lives in Santa Rosa, California with his lovely wife and three young sons.

Made in the USA
Lexington, KY
16 June 2014